NONSENSE
∴ NOVELS ∴

NONSENSE ∴NOVELS∴

BY STEPHEN LEACOCK

DOVER PUBLICATIONS, INC.

NEW YORK

This Dover edition, first published in 1971, is an unabridged and unaltered republication of the work originally published by the John Lane Company in 1912.

International Standard Book Number: 0-486-22759-6
Library of Congress Catalog Card Number: 78-166423

Manufactured in the United States of America
Dover Publications, Inc.
180 Varick Street
New York, N.Y. 10014

PREFACE

THE AUTHOR of this book offers it to the public without apology. The reviewers of his previous work of this character have presumed, on inductive grounds, that he must be a young man from the most westerly part of the Western States, to whom many things might be pardoned as due to the exuberant animal spirits of youth. They were good enough to express the thought that when the author grew up and became educated there might be hope for his intellect. This expectation is of no avail. All that education could do in this case has been tried and has failed. As a Professor of Political Economy in a great university, the author admits that he ought to know better. But he will feel amply repaid for his humiliation if there are any to whom this little book may bring some passing amusement in hours of idleness, or some brief respite when the sadness of the heart or the sufferings of the body forbid the perusal of worthier things.

STEPHEN LEACOCK

McGill University
Montreal

CONTENTS

NONSENSE
∴NOVELS∴

MADDENED BY MYSTERY:
or, The Defective Detective

THE GREAT DETECTIVE sat in his office. He wore a long green gown and half a dozen secret badges pinned to the outside of it.

Three or four pairs of false whiskers hung on a whisker-stand beside him.

Goggles, blue spectacles and motor glasses lay within easy reach.

He could completely disguise himself at a second's notice.

Half a bucket of cocaine and a dipper stood on a chair at his elbow.

His face was absolutely impenetrable.

A pile of cryptograms lay on the desk. The Great Detective hastily tore them open one after the other, solved them, and threw them down the cryptogram-shute at his side.

There was a rap at the door.

The Great Detective hurriedly wrapped himself in a pink domino, adjusted a pair of false black whiskers and cried,

"Come in."

His secretary entered. "Ha," said the detective, "it is you!"

He laid aside his disguise.

"Sir," said the young man in intense excitement, "a mystery has been committed!"

"Ha!" said the Great Detective, his eye kindling, "is it such as to completely baffle the police of the entire continent?"

"They are so completely baffled with it," said the secretary, "that they are lying collapsed in heaps; many of them have committed suicide."

"So," said the detective, "and is the mystery one that is absolutely unparalleled in the whole recorded annals of the London police?"

"It is."

"And I suppose," said the detective, "that it involves names which you would scarcely dare to breathe, at least without first using some kind of atomizer or throat-gargle."

"Exactly."

"And it is connected, I presume, with the highest diplomatic consequences, so that if we fail to solve it England will be at war with the whole world in sixteen minutes?"

His secretary, still quivering with excitement, again answered yes.

"And finally," said the Great Detective, "I presume that it was committed in broad daylight, in some such place as the entrance of the Bank of England, or in the cloak-room of the House of Commons, and under the very eyes of the police?"

"Those," said the secretary, "are the very conditions of the mystery."

"Good," said the Great Detective, "now wrap yourself in this disguise, put on these brown whiskers and tell me what it is."

The secretary wrapped himself in a blue domino with lace insertions, then, bending over, he whispered in the ear of the Great Detective:

"The Prince of Wurttemberg has been kidnapped."

The Great Detective bounded from his chair as if he had been kicked from below.

A prince stolen! Evidently a Bourbon! The scion of one of the oldest families in Europe kidnapped. Here was a mystery indeed worthy of his analytical brain.

His mind began to move like lightning.

"Stop!" he said, "how do you know this?"

The secretary handed him a telegram. It was from the Prefect of Police of Paris. It read: "The Prince of Wurttemberg stolen.

Probably forwarded to London. Must have him here for the opening day of Exhibition. £1,000 reward."

So! The Prince had been kidnapped out of Paris at the very time when his appearance at the International Exposition would have been a political event of the first magnitude.

With the Great Detective to think was to act, and to act was to think. Frequently he could do both together.

"Wire to Paris for a description of the Prince."

The secretary bowed and left.

At the same moment there was a slight scratching at the door.

A visitor entered. He crawled stealthily on his hands and knees. A hearthrug thrown over his head and shoulders disguised his identity.

He crawled to the middle of the room.

Then he rose.

Great Heaven!

It was the Prime Minister of England.

"You!" said the detective.

"Me," said the Prime Minister.

"You have come in regard to the kidnapping of the Prince of Wurttemberg?"

The Prime Minister started.

"How do you know?" he said.

The Great Detective smiled his inscrutable smile.

"Yes," said the Prime Minister. "I will use no concealment. I am interested, deeply interested. Find the Prince of Wurttemberg, get him safe back to Paris and I will add £500 to the reward already offered. But listen," he said impressively as he left the room, "see to it that no attempt is made to alter the marking of the prince, or to clip his tail."

So! To clip the Prince's tail! The brain of the Great Detective reeled. So! a gang of miscreants had conspired to—but no! the thing was not possible.

There was another rap at the door.

A second visitor was seen. He wormed his way in, lying almost prone upon his stomach, and wriggling across the floor. He was enveloped in a long purple cloak. He stood up and peeped over the top of it.

Great Heaven!

It was the Archbishop of Canterbury!

"Your Grace!" exclaimed the detective in amazement—"pray do not stand, I beg you. Sit down, lie down, anything rather than stand."

The Archbishop took off his mitre and laid it wearily on the whisker-stand.

"You are here in regard to the Prince of Wurttemberg."

The Archbishop started and crossed himself. Was the man a magician?

"Yes," he said, "much depends on getting him back. But I have only come to say this: my sister is desirous of seeing you. She is coming here. She has been extremely indiscreet and her fortune hangs upon the Prince. Get him back to Paris or I fear she will be ruined."

The Archbishop regained his mitre, uncrossed himself, wrapped his cloak about him, and crawled stealthily out on his hands and knees, purring like a cat.

The face of the Great Detective showed the most profound sympathy. It ran up and down in furrows. "So," he muttered, "the sister of the Archbishop, the Countess of Dashleigh!" Accustomed as he was to the life of the aristocracy, even the Great Detective felt that there was here intrigue of more than customary complexity.

There was a loud rapping at the door.

There entered the Countess of Dashleigh. She was all in furs.

She was the most beautiful woman in England. She strode imperiously into the room. She seized a chair imperiously and seated herself on it, imperial side up.

She took off her tiara of diamonds and put it on the tiara-holder beside her and uncoiled her boa of pearls and put in on the pearl-stand.

"You have come," said the Great Detective, "about the Prince of Wurttemburg."

"Wretched little pup!" said the Countess of Dashleigh in disgust.

So! A further complication! Far from being in love with the Prince, the Countess denounced the young Bourbon as a pup!

"You are interested in him, I believe."

"Interested!" said the Countess. "I should rather say so. Why, I bred him!"

"You which?" gasped the Great Detective, his usually impassive features suffused with a carmine blush.

"I bred him," said the Countess, "and I've got £10,000 upon his chances, so no wonder I want him back in Paris. Only listen," she said, "if they've got hold of the Prince and cut his tail or spoiled the markings of his stomach it would be far better to have him quietly put out of the way here."

The Great Detective reeled and leaned up against the side of the room. So! The cold-blooded admission of the beautiful woman for the moment took away his breath! Herself the mother of the young Bourbon, misallied with one of the greatest families of Europe, staking her fortune on a Royalist plot, and yet with so instinctive a knowledge of European politics as to know that any removal of the hereditary birth-marks of the Prince would forfeit for him the sympathy of the French populace.

The Countess resumed her tiara.

She left.

The secretary re-entered.

"I have three telegrams from Paris," he said, "they are completely baffling."

He handed over the first telegram.

It read:

"The Prince of Wurttemberg has a long, wet snout, broad ears, very long body, and short hind legs."

The Great Detective looked puzzled.

He read the second telegram.

"The Prince of Wurttemberg is easily recognized by his deep bark."

And then the third.

"The Prince of Wurttemberg can be recognized by the patch of white hair across the centre of his back."

The two men looked at one another. The mystery was maddening, impenetrable.

The Great Detective spoke.

"Give me my domino," he said. "These clues must be followed up," then pausing, while his quick brain analysed and summed up the evidence before him—"a young man," he muttered, "evidently young since described as a 'pup,' with a long, wet snout (ha! addicted obviously to drinking), a streak of white hair across his back (a first sign of the results of his abandoned life)—yes, yes," he continued, "with this clue I shall find him easily."

The Great Detective rose.

He wrapped himself in a long black cloak with white whiskers and blue spectacles attached.

Completely disguised, he issued forth.

He began the search.

For four days he visited every corner of London.

He entered every saloon in the city. In each of them he drank a glass of rum. In some of them he assumed the disguise of a sailor. In others he entered as a soldier. Into others he penetrated as a clergyman. His disguise was perfect. Nobody paid any attention to him as long as he had the price of a drink.

The search proved fruitless.

Two young men were arrested under suspicion of being the Prince, only to be released.

The identification was incomplete in each case.

One had a long wet snout but no hair on his back.

The other had hair on his back but couldn't bark.

Neither of them was the young Bourbon.

The Great Detective continued his search.

He stopped at nothing.

Secretly, after nightfall, he visited the home of the Prime Minister. He examined it from top to bottom. He measured all the doors and windows. He took up the flooring. He inspected the plumbing. He examined the furniture. He found nothing.

With equal secrecy he penetrated into the palace of the Archbishop. He examined it from top to bottom. Disguised as a choir-boy he took part in the offices of the church. He found nothing.

Still undismayed, the Great Detective made his way into the home of the Countess of Dashleigh. Disguised as a housemaid, he entered the service of the Countess.

Then at last the clue came which gave him a solution of the mystery.

On the wall of the Countess' boudoir was a large framed engraving.

It was a portrait.

Under it was a printed legend:

THE PRINCE OF WURTTEMBURG

The portrait was that of a Dachshund.

The long body, the broad ears, the unclipped tail, the short hind legs—all was there.

In the fraction of a second the lightning mind of the Great Detective had penetrated the whole mystery.

THE PRINCE WAS A DOG!!!!

Hastily throwing a domino over his housemaid's dress, he rushed to the street. He summoned a passing hansom, and in a few moments was at his house.

"I have it," he gasped to his secretary, "the mystery is solved. I have pieced it together. By sheer analysis I have reasoned it out. Listen—hind legs, hair on back, wet snout, pup—eh, what? does that suggest nothing to you?"

"Nothing," said the secretary; "it seems perfectly hopeless."

The Great Detective, now recovered from his excitement, smiled faintly.

"It means simply this, my dear fellow. The Prince of Wurttemburg is a dog, a prize Dachshund. The Countess of Dashleigh bred him, and he is worth some £25,000 in addition to the prize of £10,000 offered at the Paris dog show. Can you wonder that——"

At that moment the Great Detective was interrupted by the scream of a woman.

"Great Heaven!"

The Countess of Dashleigh dashed into the room.

Her face was wild.

Her tiara was in disorder.

Her pearls were dripping all over the place.

She wrung her hands and moaned.

"They have cut his tail," she gasped, "and taken all the hair off his back. What can I do? I am undone!!"

"Madame," said the Great Detective, calm as bronze, "do yourself up. I can save you yet."

"You!"

"Me!"

"How?"

"Listen. This is how. The Prince was to have been shown at Paris."

The Countess nodded.

"Your fortune was staked on him?"

The Countess nodded again.

"The dog was stolen, carried to London, his tail cut and his marks disfigured."

Amazed at the quiet penetration of the Great Detective, the Countess kept on nodding and nodding.

"And you are ruined?"

"I am," she gasped, and sank down on the floor in a heap of pearls.

"Madame," said the Great Detective, "all is not lost."

He straightened himself up to his full height. A look of inflinchable unflexibility flickered over his features.

The honour of England, the fortune of the most beautiful woman in England was at stake.

"I will do it," he murmured.

"Rise, dear lady," he continued. "Fear nothing. I WILL IMPERSONATE THE DOG!!!"

That night the Great Detective might have been seen on the deck of the Calais packet boat with his secretary. He was on his hands and knees in a long black cloak, and his secretary had him on a short chain.

He barked at the waves exultingly and licked the secretary's hand.

"What a beautiful dog," said the passengers.

The disguise was absolutely complete.

The Great Detective had been coated over with mucilage to which dog hairs had been applied. The markings on his back were perfect. His tail, adjusted with an automatic coupler, moved up and down responsive to every thought. His deep eyes were full of intelligence.

Next day he was exhibited in the Dachshund class at the International show.

He won all hearts.

"*Quel beau chien!*" cried the French people.

"*Ach! was ein Dog!*" cried the Spanish.

The Great Detective took the first prize!

The fortune of the Countess was saved.

Unfortunately as the Great Detective had neglected to pay the dog tax, he was caught and destroyed by the dog-catchers. But that is, of course, quite outside of the present narrative, and is only mentioned as an odd fact in conclusion.

II

"Q."

A *Psychic Pstory of the Psupernatural*

I CANNOT expect that any of my readers will believe the story which I am about to narrate. Looking back upon it, I scarcely believe it myself. Yet my narrative is so extraordinary and throws such light upon the nature of our communications with beings of another world, that I feel I am not entitled to withhold it from the public.

I had gone over to visit Annerly at his rooms. It was Saturday, October 31. I remember the date so precisely because it was my pay day, and I had received six sovereigns and ten shillings. I remember the sum so exactly because I had put the money into my pocket, and I remember into which pocket I had put it because I had no money in any other pocket. My mind is perfectly clear on all these points.

Annerly and I sat smoking for some time.

Then quite suddenly—

"Do you believe in the supernatural?" he asked.

I started as if I had been struck.

At the moment when Annerly spoke of the supernatural I had been thinking of something entirely different. The fact that he should speak of it at the very instant when I was thinking of something else, struck me as at least a very singular coincidence.

For a moment I could only stare.

"What I mean is," said Annerly, "do you believe in phantasms of the dead?"

"Phantasms?" I repeated.

"Yes, phantasms, or if you prefer the word, phanograms, or say if you will phanogrammatical manifestations, or more simply psychophantasmal phenomena?"

I looked at Annerly with a keener sense of interest than I had ever felt in him before. I felt that he was about to deal with events and experiences of which in the two or three months that I had known him he had never seen fit to speak.

I wondered now that it had never occurred to me that a man whose hair at fifty-five was already streaked with grey, must have passed through some terrible ordeal.

Presently Annerly spoke again.

"Last night I saw Q," he said.

"Good heavens!" I ejaculated. I did not in the least know who Q was, but it struck me with a thrill of indescribable terror that Annerly had seen Q. In my own quiet and measured existence such a thing had never happened.

"Yes," said Annerly, "I saw Q as plainly as if he were standing here. But perhaps I had better tell you something of my past relationship with Q, and you will understand exactly what the present situation is."

Annerly seated himself in a chair on the other side of the fire from me, lighted a pipe and continued.

"When first I knew Q he lived not very far from a small town in the south of England, which I will call X, and was betrothed to a beautiful and accomplished girl whom I will name M."

Annerly had hardly begun to speak before I found myself listening with riveted attention. I realized that it was no ordinary experience that he was about to narrate. I more than suspected the Q and M were not the real names of his unfortunate acquaintances, but were in reality two letters of the alphabet selected almost at random to disguise the names of his friends. I was still pondering over the ingenuity of the thing when Annerly went on:

"When Q and I first became friends, he had a favourite dog, which, if necessary, I might name Z, and which followed him in and out of X on his daily walk."

"In and out of X," I repeated in astonishment.

"Yes," said Annerly, "in and out."

My senses were now fully alert. That Z should have followed Q out of X, I could readily understand, but that he should first have followed him in seemed to pass the bounds of comprehension.

"Well," said Annerly, "Q and Miss M were to be married. Everything was arranged. The wedding was to take place on the last day of the year. Exactly six months and four days before the appointed day (I remember the date because the coincidence struck me as peculiar at the time) Q came to me late in the evening in great distress. He had just had, he said, a premonition of his own death. That evening, while sitting with Miss M on the verandah of her house, he had distinctly seen a projection of the dog R pass along the road."

"Stop a moment," I said. "Did you not say that the dog's name was Z?"

Annerly frowned slightly.

"Quite so," he replied. "Z, or more correctly Z R, since Q was in the habit, perhaps from motives of affection, of calling him R as well as Z. Well, then, the projection, or phanogram, of the dog passed in front of them so plainly that Miss M swore that she could have believed that it was the dog himself. Opposite the house the phantasm stopped for a moment and wagged its tail. Then it passed on, and quite suddenly disappeared around the corner of a stone wall, as if hidden by the bricks. What made the thing still more mysterious was that Miss M's mother, who is partially blind, had only partially seen the dog."

Annerly paused a moment. Then he went on:

"This singular occurrence was interpreted by Q, no doubt correctly, to indicate his own approaching death. I did what I could to remove this feeling, but it was impossible to do so, and he presently wrung my hand and left me, firmly convinced that he would not live till morning."

"Good heavens!" I exclaimed, "and he died that night?"

"No, he did not," said Annerly quietly, "that is the inexplicable part of it."

"Tell me about it," I said.

"He rose that morning as usual, dressed himself with his

customary care, omitting none of his clothes, and walked down to his office at the usual hour. He told me afterwards that he remembered the circumstances so clearly from the fact that he had gone to the office by the usual route instead of taking any other direction."

"Stop a moment," I said. "Did anything unusual happen to mark that particular day?"

"I anticipated that you would ask that question," said Annerly, "but as far as I can gather, absolutely nothing happened. Q returned from his work, and ate his dinner apparently much as usual, and presently went to bed complaining of a slight feeling of drowsiness, but nothing more. His stepmother, with whom he lived, said afterwards that she could hear the sound of his breathing quite distinctly during the night."

"And did he die that night?" I asked, breathless with excitement.

"No," said Annerly, "he did not. He rose next morning feeling about as before except that the sense of drowsiness had apparently passed, and that the sound of his breathing was no longer audible."

Annerly again fell into silence. Anxious as I was to hear the rest of his astounding narrative, I did not like to press him with questions. The fact that our relations had hitherto been only of a formal character, and that this was the first occasion on which he had invited me to visit him at his rooms, prevented me from assuming too great an intimacy.

"Well," he continued, "Q went to his office each day after that with absolute regularity. As far as I can gather there was nothing either in his surroundings or his conduct to indicate that any peculiar fate was impending over him. He saw Miss M regularly, and the time fixed for their marriage drew nearer each day."

"Each day?" I repeated in astonishment.

"Yes," said Annerly, "every day. For some time before his marriage I saw but little of him. But two weeks before that event was due to happen, I passed Q one day in the street. He seemed for a moment about to stop, then he raised his hat, smiled and passed on."

"One moment," I said, "if you will allow me a question that seems of importance—did he pass on and then smile and raise his hat, or did he smile into his hat, raise it, and then pass on afterwards?"

"Your question is quite justified," said Annerly, "though I think I can answer with perfect accuracy that he first smiled, then stopped smiling and raised his hat, and then stopped raising his hat and passed on."

"However," he continued, "the essential fact is this: on the day appointed for the wedding, Q and Miss M were duly married."

"Impossible!" I gasped; "duly married, both of them?"

"Yes," said Annerly, "both at the same time. After the wedding Mr. and Mrs. Q—"

"Mr. and Mrs. Q," I repeated in perplexity.

"Yes," he answered, "Mr. and Mrs. Q—for after the wedding Miss M took the name of Q—left England and went out to Australia, where they were to reside."

"Stop one moment," I said, "and let me be quite clear—in going out to settle in Australia it was their intention to reside there?"

"Yes," said Annerly, "that at any rate was generally understood. I myself saw them off on the steamer, and shook hands with Q, standing at the same time quite close to him."

"Well," I said, "and since the two Q's, as I suppose one might almost call them, went to Australia, have you heard anything from them?"

"That," replied Annerly, "is a matter that has shown the same singularity as the rest of my experience. It is now four years since Q and his wife went to Australia. At first I heard from him quite regularly, and received two letters each month. Presently I only received one letter every two months, and later two letters every six months, and then only one letter every twelve months. Then until last night I heard nothing whatever of Q for a year and a half."

I was now on the tiptoe of expectancy.

"Last night," said Annerly very quietly, "Q appeared in this room, or rather, a phantasm or psychic manifestation of him. He seemed in great distress, made gestures which I could not understand, and kept turning his trouser pockets inside out. I was too spellbound to question him, and tried in vain to divine his meaning. Presently the phantasm seized a pencil from the table, and wrote the words, 'Two sovereigns, to-morrow night, urgent.' "

Annerly was again silent. I sat in deep thought. "How do you interpret the meaning which Q's phanogram meant to convey?"

"I think," he announced, "it means this. Q, who is evidently dead, meant to visualize that fact, meant, so to speak, to deatomize the idea that he was demonetized, and that he wanted two sovereigns to-night."

"And how," I asked, amazed at Annerly's instinctive penetration into the mysteries of the psychic world, "how do you intend to get it to him?"

"I intend," he announced, "to try a bold, a daring experiment, which, if it succeeds, will bring us into immediate connection with the world of spirits. My plan is to leave two sovereigns here upon the edge of the table during the night. If they are gone in the morning, I shall know that Q has contrived to de-astralize himself, and has taken the sovereigns. The only question is, do you happen to have two sovereigns? I myself, unfortunately, have nothing but small change about me."

Here was a piece of rare good fortune, the coincidence of which seemed to add another link to the chain of circumstance. As it happened I had with me the six sovereigns which I had just drawn as my week's pay.

"Luckily," I said, "I am able to arrange that. I happen to have money with me." And I took two sovereigns from my pocket.

Annerly was delighted at our good luck. Our preparations for the experiment were soon made.

We placed the table in the middle of the room in such a way that there could be no fear of contact or collision with any of the furniture. The chairs were carefully set against the wall, and so placed that no two of them occupied the same place as any other two, while the pictures and ornaments about the room were left entirely undisturbed. We were careful not to remove any of the wallpaper from the wall, nor to detach any of the window-panes from the window. When all was ready the two sovereigns were laid side by side upon the table, with their heads up in such a way that the lower sides or tails were supported by only the table itself. We then extinguished the light. I said "Good night" to Annerly, and groped my way out into the dark, feverish with excitement.

My readers may well imagine my state of eagerness to know the result of the experiment. I could scarcely sleep for anxiety to know the issue. I had, of course, every faith in the completeness of our preparations, but was not without misgivings that the experiment might fail, as my own mental temperament and disposition might not be of the precise kind needed for the success of these experiments.

On this score, however, I need have had no alarm. The event showed that my mind was a media, or if the word is better, a transparency, of the very first order for psychic work of this character.

In the morning Annerly came rushing over to my lodgings, his face beaming with excitement.

"Glorious, glorious," he almost shouted, "we have succeeded! The sovereigns are gone. We are in direct monetary communication with Q."

I need not dwell on the exquisite thrill of happiness which went through me. All that day and all the following day, the sense that I was in communication with Q was ever present with me.

My only hope was that an opportunity might offer for the renewal of our intercommunication with the spirit world.

The following night my wishes were gratified. Late in the evening Annerly called me up on the telephone.

"Come over at once to my lodgings," he said. "Q's phanogram is communicating with us."

I hastened over, and arrived almost breathless. "Q has been here again," said Annerly, "and appeared in the same distress as before. A projection of him stood in the room, and kept writing with its finger on the table. I could distinguish the word 'sovereigns,' but nothing more."

"Do you not suppose," I said, "that Q for some reason which we cannot fathom, wishes us to again leave two sovereigns for him?"

"By Jove!" said Annerly enthusiastically, "I believe you've hit it. At any rate, let us try; we can but fail."

That night we placed again two of my sovereigns on the table, and arranged the furniture with the same scrupulous care as before.

Still somewhat doubtful of my own psychic fitness for the work in which I was engaged, I endeavoured to keep my mind so poised as to readily offer a mark for any astral disturbance that might be about. The result showed that it had offered just such a mark. Our experiment succeeded completely. The two coins had vanished in the morning.

For nearly two months we continued our experiments on these lines. At times Annerly himself, so he told me, would leave money, often considerable sums, within reach of the phantasm, which never failed to remove them during the night. But Annerly, being a man of strict honour, never carried on these experiments alone except when it proved impossible to communicate with me in time for me to come.

At other times he would call me up with the simple message, "Q is here," or would send me a telegram, or a written note saying, "Q needs money; bring any that you have, but no more."

On my own part, I was extremely anxious to bring our experiments prominently before the public, or to interest the Society for Psychic Research, and similar bodies, in the daring transit which we had effected between the world of sentience and the psycho-astric, or pseudo-ethereal existence. It seemed to me that we alone had succeeded in thus conveying money directly and without mediation, from one world to another. Others, indeed, had done so by the interposition of a medium, or by subscription to an occult magazine, but we had performed the feat with such simplicity that I was anxious to make our experience public, for the benefit of others like myself.

Annerly, however, was averse from this course, being fearful that it might break off our relations with Q.

It was some three months after our first inter-astral psycho-monetary experiment, that there came the culmination of my experiences—so mysterious as to leave me still lost in perplexity.

Annerly had come in to see me one afternoon. He looked nervous and depressed.

"I have just had a psychic communication from Q," he said in answer to my inquiries, "which I can hardly fathom. As far as I can judge, Q has formed some plan for interesting other phantasms in the kind of work that we are doing. He proposes to form, on his side of the gulf, an association that is to work in harmony with us, for monetary dealings on a large scale, between the two worlds."

My reader may well imagine that my eyes almost blazed with excitement at the magnitude of the prospect opened up.

"Q wishes us to gather together all the capital that we can, and to send it across to him, in order that he may be able to organize with him a corporate association of phanograms, or perhaps in this case, one would more correctly call them phantoids."

I had no sooner grasped Annerly's meaning than I became enthusiastic over it.

We decided to try the great experiment that night.

My own worldly capital was, unfortunately, no great amount. I had, however, some £500 in bank stock left to me at my father's decease, which I could, of course, realize within a few hours. I was fearful, however, lest it might prove too small to enable Q to organize his fellow phantoids with it.

I carried the money in notes and sovereigns to Annerly's room, where it was laid on the table. Annerly was fortunately able to contribute a larger sum, which, however, he was not to place beside mine until after I had withdrawn, in order that conjunction of our monetary personalities might not dematerialize the astral phenomenon.

We made our preparations this time with exceptional care, Annerly quietly confident, I, it must be confessed, extremely nervous and fearful of failure. We removed our boots, and walked about on our stockinged feet, and at Annerly's suggestion, not only placed the furniture as before, but turned the coal-scuttle upside down, and laid a wet towel over the top of the wastepaper basket.

All complete, I wrung Annerly's hand, and went out into the darkness.

I waited next morning in vain. Nine o'clock came, ten o'clock, and finally eleven, and still no word of him. Then feverish with anxiety, I sought his lodgings.

Judge of my utter consternation to find that Annerly had disappeared. He had vanished as if off the face of the earth. By what awful error in our preparations, by what neglect of some necessary psychic precautions, he had met his fate, I cannot tell. But the evidence was only too clear, that Annerly had been engulfed into the astral world, carrying with him the money for the transfer of which he had risked his mundane existence.

The proof of his disappearance was easy to find. As soon as I dared do so with discretion I ventured upon a few inquiries. The fact that he had been engulfed while still owing four month's rent for his rooms, and that he had vanished without even having time to pay such bills as he had outstanding with local tradesmen, showed that he must have been devisualized at a moment's notice.

The awful fear that I might be held accountable for his death, prevented me from making the affair public.

Till that moment I had not realized the risks that he had incurred in our reckless dealing with the world of spirits. Annerly fell a victim to the great cause of psychic science, and the record of our experiments remain in the face of prejudice as a witness to its truth.

III

GUIDO THE GIMLET OF GHENT:
A Romance of Chivalry

IT WAS in the flood-tide of chivalry. Knighthood was in the pod.

The sun was slowly setting in the east, rising and falling occasionally as it subsided, and illuminating with its dying beams the towers of the grim castle of Buggensberg.

Isolde the Slender stood upon an embattled turret of the castle. Her arms were outstretched to the empty air, and her face, upturned as if in colloquy with heaven, was distraught with yearning.

Anon she murmured, "Guido"—and bewhiles a deep sigh rent her breast.

Sylph-like and ethereal in her beauty, she scarcely seemed to breathe.

In fact she hardly did.

Willowy and slender in form, she was as graceful as a meridian of longitude. Her body seemed almost too frail for motion, while her features were of a mould so delicate as to preclude all thought of intellectual operation.

She was begirt with a flowing kirtle of deep blue, bebound with a belt bebuckled with a silvern clasp, while about her waist a stomacher of point lace ended in the ruffled farthingale at her throat. On her head she bore a sugarloaf hat shaped like an extinguisher and pointing backward at an angle of 45 degrees.

"Guido," she murmured, "Guido."

And erstwhile she would wring her hands as one distraught and mutter, "He cometh not."

The sun sank and night fell, enwrapping in shadow the frowning castle of Buggensberg, and the ancient city of Ghent at its foot. And as the darkness gathered, the windows of the castle shone out with fiery red, for it was Yuletide, and it was wassail all in the Great Hall of the castle, and this night the Margrave of Buggensberg made him a feast, and celebrated the betrothal of Isolde, his daughter, with Tancred the Tenspot.

And to the feast he had bidden all his liege lords and vassals—Hubert the Husky, Edward the Earwig, Rollo the Rumbottle, and many others.

In the meantime the Lady Isolde stood upon the battlements and mourned for the absent Guido.

The love of Guido and Isolde was of that pure and almost divine type, found only in the middle ages.

They had never seen one another. Guido had never seen Isolde, Isolde had never seen Guido. They had never heard one another speak. They had never been together. They did not know one another.

Yet they loved.

Their love had sprung into being suddenly and romantically, with all the mystic charm which is love's greatest happiness.

Years before, Guido had seen the name of Isolde the Slender painted on a fence.

He had turned pale, fallen into a swoon and started at once for Jerusalem.

On the very same day Isolde in passing through the streets of Ghent had seen the coat of arms of Guido hanging on a clothes line.

She had fallen back into the arms of her tire-women more dead than alive.

Since that day they had loved.

Isolde would wander forth from the castle at earliest morn, with the name of Guido on her lips. She told his name to the trees. She whispered it to the flowers. She breathed it to the birds. Quite a lot of them knew it. At times she would ride her palfrey along the sands of the sea and call "Guido" to the waves! At other times she would tell it to the grass or even to a stick of cordwood or a ton of coal.

Guido and Isolde, though they had never met, cherished each the features of the other. Beneath his coat of mail Guido carried a miniature of Isolde, carven on ivory. He had found it at the bottom of the castle crag, between the castle and the old town of Ghent at its foot.

How did he know that it was Isolde?

There was no need for him to ask.

His *heart* had spoken.

The eye of love cannot be deceived.

And Isolde? She, too, cherished beneath her stomacher a miniature of Guido the Gimlet. She had it of a travelling chapman in whose pack she had discovered it, and had paid its price in pearls. How had she known that he it was, that is, that it was he? Because of the Coat of Arms emblazoned beneath the miniature. The same heraldic design that had first shaken her to the heart. Sleeping or waking it was ever before her eyes: A lion, proper, quartered in a field of gules, and a dog, improper, three-quarters in a field of buckwheat.

And if the love of Isolde burned thus purely for Guido, the love of Guido burned for Isolde with a flame no less pure.

No sooner had love entered Guido's heart than he had determined to do some great feat of emprise or adventure, some high achievement of deringdo which should make him worthy to woo her.

He placed himself under a vow that he would eat nothing, save only food, and drink nothing, save only liquor, till such season as he should have performed his feat.

For this cause he had at once set out for Jerusalem to kill a Saracen for her. He killed one, quite a large one. Still under his vow, he set out again at once to the very confines of Pannonia determined to kill a Turk for her. From Pannonia he passed into the Highlands of Britain, where he killed her a Caledonian.

Every year and every month Guido performed for Isolde some new achievement of emprise.

And in the meantime Isolde waited.

It was not that suitors were lacking. Isolde the Slender had suitors in plenty ready to do her lightest hest.

Feats of arms were done daily for her sake. To win her love suitors were willing to vow themselves to perdition. For Isolde's sake, Otto the Otter had cast himself into the sea. Conrad the Cocoanut had hurled himself from the highest battlement of the castle head first into the mud. Hugo the Hopeless had hanged himself by the waistband to a hickory tree and had refused all efforts to dislodge him. For her sake Siegfried the Susceptible had swallowed sulphuric acid.

But Isolde the Slender was heedless of the court thus paid to her.

In vain her stepmother, Agatha the Angular, urged her to marry. In vain her father, the Margrave of Buggensberg, commanded her to choose the one or the other of the suitors.

Her heart remained unswervingly true to the Gimlet.

From time to time love tokens passed between the lovers. From Jerusalem Guido had sent to her a stick with a notch in it to signify his undying constancy. From Pannonia he sent a piece of board, and from Venetia about two feet of scantling. All these Isolde treasured. At night they lay beneath her pillow.

Then, after years of wandering, Guido had determined to crown his love with a final achievement for Isolde's sake.

It was his design to return to Ghent, to scale by night the castle cliff and to prove his love for Isolde by killing her father for her, casting her stepmother from the battlements, burning the castle, and carrying her away.

This design he was now hastening to put into execution. Attended by fifty trusty followers under the lead of Carlo the Corkscrew and Beowulf the Bradawl, he had made his way to Ghent. Under cover of night they had reached the foot of the castle cliff; and now, on their hands and knees in single file, they were crawling round and round the spiral path that led up to the gate of the fortress. At six of the clock they had spiralled once. At seven of the clock they had reappeared at the second round, and as the feast in the hall reached its height, they reappeared on the fourth lap.

Guido the Gimlet was in the lead. His coat of mail was hidden beneath a parti-coloured cloak and he bore in his hand a horn.

By arrangement he was to penetrate into the castle by the postern gate in disguise, steal from the Margrave by artifice the key of the great door, and then by a blast of his horn summon his followers to the assault. Alas! there was need for haste, for at this very Yuletide, on this very night, the Margrave, wearied of Isolde's resistance, had determined to bestow her hand upon Tancred the Tenspot.

It was wassail all in the great hall. The huge Margrave, seated at the head of the board, drained flagon after flagon of wine, and pledged deep the health of Tancred the Tenspot, who sat plumed and armoured beside him.

Great was the merriment of the Margrave, for beside him, crouched upon the floor, was a new jester, whom the seneschal had just admitted by the postern gate, and the novelty of whose jests made the huge sides of the Margrave shake and shake again.

"Odds Bodikins!" he roared, "but the tale is as rare as it is new! and so the wagoner said to the Pilgrim that sith he had asked him to put him off the wagon in that town, put him off he must, albeit it was but the small of the night—by St. Pancras! whence hath the fellow so novel a tale?—nay, tell it me but once more, haply I may remember it"—and the Baron fell back in a perfect paroxysm of merriment.

As he fell back, Guido—for the disguised jester was none other than he, that is, than him—sprang forward and seized from the girdle of the Margrave the key of the great door that dangled at his waist.

Then, casting aside the jester's cloak and cap, he rose to his full height, standing in his coat of mail.

In one hand he brandished the double-headed mace of the Crusader, and in the other a horn.

The guests sprang to their feet, their hands upon their daggers.

"Guido the Gimlet!" they cried.

"Hold," said Guido, "I have you in my power!!"

Then placing the horn to his lips and drawing a deep breath, he blew with his utmost force.

And then again he blew—blew like anything.

Not a sound came.

The horn wouldn't blow!

"Seize him!" cried the Baron.

"Stop," said Guido, "I claim the laws of chivalry. I am here to seek the Lady Isolde, betrothed by you to Tancred. Let me fight Tancred in single combat, man to man."

A shout of approbation gave consent.

The combat that followed was terrific.

First Guido, raising his mace high in the air with both hands, brought it down with terrible force on Tancred's mailed head. Then Guido stood still, and Tancred raising his mace in the air brought it down upon Guido's head. Then Tancred stood still and turned his back, and Guido, swinging his mace sideways, gave him a terrific blow from behind, midway, right centre. Tancred returned the blow. Then Tancred knelt down on his hands and knees and Guido brought the mace down on his back. It was a sheer contest of skill and agility. For a time the issue was doubtful. Then Tancred's armour began to bend, his blows weakened, he fell prone. Guido pressed his advantage and hammered him out as flat as a sardine can. Then placing his foot on Tancred's chest, he lowered his vizor and looked around about him.

At this second there was a resounding shriek.

Isolde the Slender, alarmed by the sound of the blows, precipitated herself into the room.

For a moment the lovers looked into each other's faces.

Then with their countenances distraught with agony they fell swooning in different directions.

There had been a mistake!

Guido was not Guido, and Isolde was not Isolde. They were

wrong about the miniatures. Each of them was a picture of somebody else.

Torrents of remorse flooded over the lovers' hearts.

Isolde thought of the unhappy Tancred, hammered out as flat as a picture-card and hopelessly spoilt; of Conrad the Cocoanut head first in the mud, and Sickfried the Susceptible coiled up with agonies of sulphuric acid.

Guido thought of the dead Saracens and the slaughtered Turks.

And all for nothing!

The guerdon of their love had proved vain. Each of them was not what the other had thought. So it is ever with the loves of this world, and herein is the medieval allegory of this tale.

The hearts of the two lovers broke together.

They expired.

Meantime Carlo the Corkscrew and Beowulf the Bradawl, and their forty followers, were hustling down the spirals as fast as they could crawl, hind end uppermost.

IV

GERTRUDE THE GOVERNESS:

or, Simple Seventeen

Synopsis of Previous Chapters:
There are no Previous Chapters

IT WAS A wild and stormy night on the West Coast of Scotland. This, however, is immaterial to the present story, as the scene is not laid in the West of Scotland. For the matter of that the weather was just as bad on the East Coast of Ireland.

But the scene of this narrative is laid in the South of England and takes place in and around Knotacentinum Towers (pronounced as if written Nosham Taws), the seat of Lord Knotacent (pronounced as if written Nosh).

But it is not necessary to pronounce either of these names in reading them.

Nosham Taws was a typical English home. The main part of the house was an Elizabethan structure of warm red brick, while the elder portion, of which the Earl was inordinately proud, still showed the outlines of a Norman Keep, to which had been added a Lancastrian Jail and a Plantagenet Orphan Asylum. From the house in all directions stretched magnificent woodland and park with oaks and elms of immemorial antiquity, while nearer the house stood raspberry bushes and geranium plants which had been set out by the Crusaders.

About the grand old mansion the air was loud with the chirping of thrushes, the cawing of partridges and the clear sweet note of the rook, while deer, antelope and other quadrupeds strutted about the lawn so tame as to eat off the sun-dial. In fact, the place was a regular menagerie.

From the house downwards through the park stretched a beautiful broad avenue laid out by Henry VII.

Lord Nosh stood upon the hearthrug of the library. Trained diplomat and statesman as he was, his stern aristocratic face was upside down with fury.

"Boy," he said, "you shall marry this girl or I disinherit you. You are no son of mine."

Young Lord Ronald, erect before him, flung back a glance as defiant as his own.

"I defy you," he said. "Henceforth you are no father of mine. I will get another. I will marry none but a woman I can love. This girl that we have never seen——"

"Fool," said the Earl, "would you throw aside our estate and name of a thousand years? The girl, I am told, is beautiful; her aunt is willing; they are French; pah! they understand such things in France."

"But your reason——"

"I give no reason," said the Earl. "Listen, Ronald, I give one month. For that time you remain here. If at the end of it you refuse me, I cut you off with a shilling."

Lord Ronald said nothing; he flung himself from the room, flung himself upon his horse and rode madly off in all directions.

As the door of the library closed upon Ronald, the Earl sank into a chair. His face changed. It was no longer that of the haughty nobleman, but of the hunted criminal. "He must marry the girl," he muttered. "Soon she will know all. Tutchemoff has escaped from Siberia. He knows and will tell. The whole of the mines pass to her, this property with it, and I—but enough." He rose, walked to the sideboard, drained a dipper full of gin and bitters, and became again a high-bred English gentleman.

It was at this moment that a high dogcart, driven by a groom in the livery of Earl Nosh, might have been seen entering the avenue of Nosham Taws. Beside him sat a young girl, scarce more than a child, in fact not nearly so big as the groom.

The apple-pie hat which she wore, surmounted with black

willow plumes, concealed from view a face so face-like in its appearance as to be positively facial.

It was—need we say it—Gertrude the Governess, who was this day to enter upon her duties at Nosham Taws.

At the same time that the dogcart entered the avenue at one end there might have been seen riding down it from the other a tall young man, whose long, aristocratic face proclaimed his birth and who was mounted upon a horse with a face even longer than his own.

And who is this tall young man who draws nearer to Gertrude with every revolution of the horse? Ah, who, indeed? Ah, who, who? I wonder if any of my readers could guess that this was none other than Lord Ronald.

The two were destined to meet. Nearer and nearer they came. And then still nearer. Then for one brief moment they met. As they passed Gertrude raised her head and directed towards the young nobleman two eyes so eye-like in their expression as to be absolutely circular, while Lord Ronald directed towards the occupant of the dogcart a gaze so gaze-like that nothing but a gazelle, or a gas-pipe, could have emulated its intensity.

Was this the dawn of love? Wait and see. Do not spoil the story.

Let us speak of Gertrude. Gertrude DeMongmorenci McFiggin had known neither father nor mother. They had both died years before she was born. Of her mother she knew nothing, save that she was French, was extremely beautiful, and that all her ancestors and even her business acquaintances had perished in the Revolution.

Yet Gertrude cherished the memory of her parents. On her breast the girl wore a locket in which was enshrined a miniature of her mother, while down her neck inside at the back hung a daguerreotype of her father. She carried a portrait of her grandmother up her sleeve and had pictures of her cousins tucked inside her boot, while beneath her—but enough, quite enough.

Of her father Gertrude knew even less. That he was a high-born

English gentleman who had lived as a wanderer in many lands, this was all she knew. His only legacy to Gertrude had been a Russian grammar, a Roumanian phrase-book, a theodolite, and a work on mining engineering.

From her earliest infancy Gertrude had been brought up by her aunt. Her aunt had carefully instructed her in Christian principles. She had also taught her Mohammedanism to make sure.

When Gertrude was seventeen her aunt had died of hydrophobia.

The circumstances were mysterious. There had called upon her that day a strange bearded man in the costume of the Russians. After he had left, Gertrude had found her aunt in a syncope from which she passed into an apostrophe and never recovered.

To avoid scandal it was called hydrophobia. Gertrude was thus thrown upon the world. What to do? That was the problem that confronted her.

It was while musing one day upon her fate that Gertrude's eye was struck with an advertisement.

"Wanted a governess; must possess a knowledge of French, Italian, Russian, and Roumanian, Music, and Mining Engineering. Salary £1,4 shillings and 4 pence halfpenny per annum. Apply between half-past eleven and twenty-five minutes to twelve at No. 41 A Decimal Six, Belgravia Terrace. The Countess of Nosh."

Gertrude was a girl of great natural quickness of apprehension, and she had not pondered over this announcement more than half an hour before she was struck with the extraordinary coincidence between the list of items desired and the things that she herself knew.

She duly presented herself at Belgravia Terrace before the Countess, who advanced to meet her with a charm which at once placed the girl at her ease.

"You are proficient in French," she asked.

"*Oh, oui*," said Gertrude modestly.

"And Italian," continued the Countess.

"*Oh, si*," said Gertrude.

"And Russian?"

"*Yaw.*"

"And Roumanian?"

"*Jep.*"

Amazed at the girl's extraordinary proficiency in modern languages, the Countess looked at her narrowly. Where had she seen those lineaments before? She passed her hand over her brow in thought, and spit upon the floor, but no, the face baffled her.

"Enough," she said, "I engage you on the spot; to-morrow you go down to Nosham Taws and begin teaching the children. I must add that in addition you will be expected to aid the Earl with his Russian correspondence. He has large mining interests at Tschminsk."

Tschminsk! why did the simple word reverberate upon Gertrude's ears? Why? Because it was the name written in her father's hand on the title page of his book on mining. What mystery was here?

It was on the following day that Gertrude had driven up the avenue.

She descended from the dogcart, passed through a phalanx of liveried servants drawn up seven-deep, to each of whom she gave a sovereign as she passed and entered Nosham Taws.

"Welcome," said the Countess, as she aided Gertrude to carry her trunk upstairs.

The girl presently descended and was ushered into the library, where she was presented to the Earl. As soon as the Earl's eye fell upon the face of the new governess he started visibly. Where had he seen those lineaments? Where was it? At the races, or the theatre—on a bus—no. Some subtler thread of memory was stirring in his mind. He strode hastily to the sideboard, drained a dipper and a half of brandy, and became again the perfect English gentleman.

While Gertrude has gone to the nursery to make the acquaintance of the two tiny golden-haired children who are to be her charges, let us say something here of the Earl and his son.

Lord Nosh was the perfect type of the English nobleman and statesman. The years that he had spent in the diplomatic service at Constantinople, St. Petersburg, and Salt Lake City had given to him a peculiar finesse and noblesse, while his long residence at St. Helena, Pitcairn Island, and Hamilton, Ontario, had rendered him impervious to external impressions. As deputy-paymaster of the militia of the county he had seen something of the sterner side of military life, while his hereditary office of Groom of the Sunday Breeches had brought him into direct contact with Royalty itself.

His passion for outdoor sports endeared him to his tenants. A keen sportsman, he excelled in fox-hunting, dog-hunting, pig-killing, bat-catching and the pastimes of his class.

In this latter respect Lord Ronald took after his father. From the start the lad had shown the greatest promise. At Eton he had made a splendid showing at battledore and shuttlecock, and at Cambridge had been first in his class at needlework. Already his name was whispered in connection with the All England ping-pong championship, a triumph which would undoubtedly carry with it a seat in Parliament.

Thus was Gertrude the Governess installed at Nosham Taws.

The days and the weeks sped past.

The simple charm of the beautiful orphan girl attracted all hearts. Her two little pupils became her slaves. "Me loves oo," little Rasehellfrida would say, leaning her golden head in Gertrude's lap. Even the servants loved her. The head gardener would bring a bouquet of beautiful roses to her room before she was up, the second gardener a bunch of early cauliflowers, the third a spray of late asparagus, and even the tenth and eleventh a sprig of mangel-wurzel or an armful of hay. Her room was full of gardeners all the time, while at evening the aged butler, touched at the friendless girl's loneliness, would tap softly at her door to bring her a rye whisky and seltzer or a box of Pittsburg Stogies. Even the dumb creatures seemed to admire her in their own dumb way. The dumb rooks settled on her shoulder and every dumb dog around the place followed her.

And Ronald! ah, Ronald! Yes, indeed! They had met. They had spoken.

"What a dull morning," Gertrude had said. *"Quel triste matin! Was fur ein allerverdamnter Tag!"*

"Beastly," Ronald had answered.

"Beastly!!" The word rang in Gertrude's ears all day.

After that they were constantly together. They played tennis and ping-pong in the day, and in the evening, in accordance with the stiff routine of the place, they sat down with the Earl and Countess to twenty-five-cent poker, and later still they sat together on the verandah and watched the moon sweeping in great circles around the horizon.

It was not long before Gertrude realized that Lord Ronald felt towards her a warmer feeling than that of mere ping-pong. At times in her presence he would fall, especially after dinner, into a fit of profound subtraction.

Once at night, when Gertrude withdrew to her chamber and before seeking her pillow, prepared to retire as a preliminary to disrobing—in other words, before going to bed, she flung wide the casement (opened the window) and perceived (saw) the face of Lord Ronald. He was sitting on a thorn bush beneath her, and his upturned face wore an expression of agonized pallor.

Meantime the days passed. Life at the Taws moved in the ordinary routine of a great English household. At 7 a gong sounded for rising, at 8 a horn blew for breakfast, at 8.30 a whistle sounded for prayers, at 1 a flag was run up at half-mast for lunch, at 4 a gun was fired for afternoon tea, at 9 a first bell sounded for dressing, at 9.15 a second bell for going on dressing, while at 9.30 a rocket was sent up to indicate that dinner was ready. At midnight dinner was over, and at 1 a.m. the tolling of a bell summoned the domestics to evening prayers.

Meanwhile the month allotted by the Earl to Lord Ronald was passing away. It was already July 15, then within a day or two it was July 17, and, almost immediately afterwards, July 18.

At times the Earl, in passing Ronald in the hall, would say sternly, "Remember, boy, your consent, or I disinherit you."

And what were the Earl's thoughts of Gertrude? Here was the

one drop of bitterness in the girl's cup of happiness. For some reason that she could not divine the Earl showed signs of marked antipathy.

Once as she passed the door of the library he threw a bootjack at her. On another occasion at lunch alone with her he struck her savagely across the face with a sausage.

It was her duty to translate to the Earl his Russian correspondence. She sought in it in vain for the mystery. One day a Russian telegram was handed to the Earl. Gertrude translated it to him aloud.

"Tutchemoff went to the woman. She is dead."

On hearing this the Earl became livid with fury, in fact this was the day that he struck her with the sausage.

Then one day while the Earl was absent on a bat hunt, Gertrude, who was turning over his correspondence, with that sweet feminine instinct of interest that rose superior to ill-treatment, suddenly found the key to the mystery.

Lord Nosh was not the rightful owner of the Taws. His distant cousin of the older line, the true heir, had died in a Russian prison to which the machinations of the Earl, while Ambassador at Tschminsk, had consigned him. The daughter of this cousin was the true owner of Nosham Taws.

The family story, save only that the documents before her withheld the name of the rightful heir, lay bare to Gertrude's eye.

Strange is the heart of woman. Did Gertrude turn from the Earl with spurning? No. Her own sad fate had taught her sympathy.

Yet still the mystery remained! Why did the Earl start perceptibly each time that he looked into her face? Sometimes he started as much as four centimetres, so that one could distinctly see him do it. On such occasions he would hastily drain a dipper of rum and vichy water and become again the correct English gentleman.

The denouement came swiftly. Gertrude never forgot it.

It was the night of the great ball at Nosham Taws. The whole neighbourhood was invited. How Gertrude's heart had beat with anticipation, and with what trepidation she had overhauled her scant wardrobe in order to appear not unworthy in Lord Ronald's eyes. Her resources were poor indeed, yet the inborn genius for dress that she inherited from her French mother stood her in good stead. She twined a single rose in her hair and contrived herself a dress out of a few old newspapers and the inside of an umbrella that would have graced a court. Round her waist she bound a single braid of bagstring, while a piece of old lace that had been her mother's was suspended to her ear by a thread.

Gertrude was the cynosure of all eyes. Floating to the strains of the music she presented a picture of bright girlish innocence that no one could see undisenraptured.

The ball was at its height. It was away up!

Ronald stood with Gertrude in the shrubbery. They looked into one another's eyes.

"Gertrude," he said, "I love you."

Simple words, and yet they thrilled every fibre in the girl's costume.

"Ronald!" she said, and cast herself about his neck.

At this moment the Earl appeared standing beside them in the moonlight. His stern face was distorted with indignation.

"So!" he said, turning to Ronald, "it appears that you have chosen!"

"I have," said Ronald with hauteur.

"You prefer to marry this penniless girl rather than the heiress I have selected for you."

Gertrude looked from father to son in amazement.

"Yes," said Ronald.

"Be it so," said the Earl, draining a dipper of gin which he carried, and resuming his calm.

"Then I disinherit you. Leave this place, and never return to it."

"Come, Gertrude," said Ronald tenderly, "let us flee together."

Gertrude stood before them. The rose had fallen from her head. The lace had fallen from her ear and the bagstring had come undone from her waist. Her newspapers were crumpled beyond recognition. But dishevelled and illegible as she was, she was still mistress of herself.

"Never," she said firmly. "Ronald, you shall never make this sacrifice for me." Then to the Earl, in tones of ice, "There is a pride, sir, as great even as yours. The daughter of Metschnikoff McFiggin need crave a boon from no one."

With that she hauled from her bosom the daguerreotype of her father and pressed it to her lips.

The Earl started as if shot. "That name!" he cried, "that face! that photograph! stop!"

There! There is no need to finish; my readers have long since divined it. Gertrude was the heiress.

The lovers fell into one another's arms. The Earl's proud face relaxed. "God bless you," he said. The Countess and the guests came pouring out upon the lawn. The breaking day illuminated a scene of gay congratulations.

Gertrude and Ronald were wed. Their happiness was complete. Need we say more? Yes, only this. The Earl was killed in the hunting-field a few days after. The Countess was struck by lightning. The two children fell down a well. Thus the happiness of Gertrude and Ronald was complete.

V

A HERO IN HOMESPUN:

or, The Life Struggle of Hezekiah Hayloft

CAN YOU give me a job?"

The foreman of the bricklayers looked down from the scaffold to the speaker below. Something in the lad's upturned face appealed to the man. He threw a brick at him.

It was Hezekiah Hayloft. He was all in homespun. He carried a carpet-bag in each hand. He had come to New York, the cruel city, looking for work.

Hezekiah moved on. Presently he stopped in front of a policeman.

"Sir," he said, "can you tell me the way to——"

The policeman struck him savagely across the side of the head.

"I'll learn you," he said, "to ask damn fool questions——"

Again Hezekiah moved on. In a few moments he met a man whose tall black hat, black waistcoat and white tie proclaimed him a clergyman.

"Good sir," said Hezekiah, "can you tell me——"

The clergyman pounced upon him with a growl of a hyena, and bit a piece out of his ear. Yes, he did, reader. Just imagine a clergyman biting a boy in open daylight! Yet that happens in New York every minute.

Such is the great cruel city, and imagine looking for work in it. You and I who spend our time in trying to avoid work can hardly realize what it must mean. Think how it must feel to be alone in New York, without a friend or a relation at hand, with no one to know or care what you do. It must be great!

For a few moments Hezekiah stood irresolute. He looked about him. He looked up at the top of the Metropolitan Tower. He saw no work there. He looked across at the sky-scrapers on Madison Square, but his eye detected no work in any of them. He stood on his head and looked up at the flat-iron building. Still no work in sight.

All that day and the next Hezekiah looked for work.

A Wall Street firm had advertised for a stenographer.

"Can you write shorthand?" they said.

"No," said the boy in homespun, "but I can try."

They threw him down the elevator.

Hezekiah was not discouraged. That day he applied for fourteen jobs.

The Waldorf Astoria was in need of a chef. Hezekiah applied for the place.

"Can you cook?" they said.

"No," said Hezekiah, "but oh, sir, give me a trial, give me an egg and let me try—I will try so hard." Great tears rolled down the boy's face.

They rolled him out into the corridor.

Next he applied for a job as a telegrapher. His mere ignorance of telegraphy was made the ground of refusal.

At nightfall Hezekiah Hayloft grew hungry. He entered again the portico of the Waldorf Astoria. Within it stood a tall man in uniform.

"Boss," said the boy hero, "will you trust me for the price of a square meal?"

They set the dog on him.

Such, reader, is the hardness and bitterness of the Great City.

For fourteen weeks Hezekiah Hayloft looked for work. Once or twice he obtained temporary employment only to lose it again.

For a few days he was made accountant in a trust company. He was discharged because he would not tell a lie. For about a week he held a position as cashier in a bank. They discharged the lad because he refused to forge a cheque. For three days he held a conductorship on a Broadway surface car. He was dismissed from this business for refusing to steal a nickle.

Such, reader, is the horrid degradation of business life in New York.

Meantime the days passed and still Hayloft found no work. His stock of money was exhausted. He had not had any money anyway. For food he ate grass in Central Park and drank the water from the Cruelty to Animals horsetrough.

Gradually a change came over the lad; his face grew hard and stern, the great city was setting its mark upon him.

One night Hezekiah stood upon the sidewalk. It was late, long after ten o'clock. Only a few chance pedestrians passed.

"By Heaven!" said Hezekiah, shaking his fist at the lights of the cruel city, "I have exhausted fair means, I will try foul. I will beg. No Hayloft has been a beggar yet," he added with a bitter laugh, "but I will begin."

A well-dressed man passed along.

Hezekiah seized him by the throat.

"What do you want?" cried the man in sudden terror. "Don't ask me for work. I tell you I have no work to give."

"I don't want work," said Hezekiah grimly. "I am a beggar."

"Oh! is that all," said the man, relieved. "Here, take this ten dollars and go and buy a drink with it."

Money! money! and with it a new sense of power that rushed like an intoxicant to Hezekiah's brain.

"Drink," he muttered hoarsely, "yes, drink."

The lights of a soda-water fountain struck his eye.

"Give me an egg phosphate," he said as he dashed his money on the counter. He drank phosphate after phosphate till his brain reeled. Mad with the liquor, he staggered to and fro in the shop, weighed himself recklessly on the slot machine three or four times, tore out chewing gum and matches from the automatic nickel boxes, and finally staggered on to the street, reeling from the effects of thirteen phosphates and a sarsaparilla soda.

"Crime," he hissed. "Crime, crime, that's what I want."

He noticed that the passers-by made way for him now with respect. On the corner of the street a policeman was standing.

Hezekiah picked up a cobblestone, threw it, and struck the man full on the ear.

The policeman smiled at him roguishly, and then gently wagged his finger in reproof. It was the same policeman who had struck him fourteen weeks before for asking the way.

Hezekiah moved on, still full of his new idea of crime. Down the street was a novelty shop, the window decked with New Year's gifts.

"Sell me a revolver," he said.

"Yes, sir," said the salesman. "Would you like something for evening wear, or a plain kind for home use. Here is a very good family revolver, or would you like a roof garden size?"

Hezekiah selected a revolver and went out.

"Now, then," he muttered, "I will burglarize a house and get money."

Walking across to Fifth Avenue he selected one of the finest residences and rang the bell.

A man in livery appeared in the brightly lighted hall.

"Where is your master?" Hezekiah asked, showing his revolver.

"He is upstairs, sir, counting his money," the man answered, "but he dislikes being disturbed."

"Show me to him," said Hezekiah, "I wish to shoot him and take his money."

"Very good, sir," said the man deferentially. "You will find him on the first floor."

Hezekiah turned and shot the footman twice through the livery and went upstairs.

In an upper room was a man sitting at a desk under a reading-lamp. In front of him was a pile of gold.

He was an old man, with a foolish, benevolent face.

"What are you doing?" said Hezekiah.

"I am counting my money," said the man.

"What are you?" asked Hezekiah sternly.

"I am a philanthropist," said the man. "I give my money to deserving objects. I establish medals for heroes. I give prizes for ship captains who jump into the sea, and for firemen who throw people from the windows of upper stories at the risk of their own; I send American missionaries to China, Chinese missionaries to India, and Indian missionaries to Chicago. I set aside money to keep college professors from starving to death when they deserve it."

"Stop!" said Hezekiah, "you deserve to die. Stand up. Open your mouth and shut your eyes."

The old man stood up.

There was a loud report. The philanthropist fell. He was shot through the waistcoat and his suspenders were cut to ribbons.

Hezekiah, his eyes glittering with the mania of crime, crammed his pockets with gold pieces.

There was a roar and hubbub in the street below.

"The police!" Hezekiah muttered. "I must set fire to the house and escape in the confusion."

He struck a safety match and held it to the leg of the table.

It was a fireproof table and refused to burn. He held it to the door. The door was fireproof. He applied it to the bookcase. He ran the match along the books. They were all fireproof. Everything was fireproof.

Frenzied with rage, he tore off his celluloid collar and set fire to it. He waved it above his head. Great tongues of flame swept from the windows.

"Fire! Fire!" was the cry.

Hezekiah rushed to the door and threw the blazing collar down the elevator shaft. In a moment the iron elevator, with its steel ropes, burst into a mass of flame; then the brass fittings of the doors took fire, and in a moment the cement floor of the elevator was one roaring mass of flame. Great columns of smoke burst from the building.

"Fire! Fire!" shouted the crowd.

Reader, have you ever seen a fire in a great city? The sight is a wondrous one. One realizes that, vast and horrible as the city is, it nevertheless shows its human organization in its most perfect form.

Scarcely had the fire broken out before resolute efforts were made to stay its progress. Long lines of men passed buckets of water from hand to hand.

The water was dashed on the fronts of the neighbouring houses, thrown all over the street, splashed against the telegraph poles, and poured in torrents over the excited crowd. Every place in the neighbourhood of the fire was literally soaked. The men worked with a will. A derrick rapidly erected in the street reared itself to the height of sixteen or seventeen feet. A daring man mounted on the top of it, hauled bucket after bucket of water on the pulley. Balancing himself with the cool daring of the trained fireman, he threw the water in all directions over the crowd.

The fire raged for an hour. Hezekiah, standing at an empty window amid the flames, rapidly filled his revolver and emptied it into the crowd.

From one hundred revolvers in the street a fusillade was kept up in return.

This lasted for an hour. Several persons were almost hit by the rain of bullets, which would have proved fatal had they struck anyone.

Meantime, as the flames died down, a squad of policemen rushed into the doomed building.

Hezekiah threw aside his revolver and received them with folded arms.

"Hayloft," said the chief of police, "I arrest you for murder, burglary, arson, and conspiracy. You put up a splendid fight, old man, and I am only sorry that it is our painful duty to arrest you."

As Hayloft appeared below a great cheer went up from the crowd. True courage always appeals to the heart of the people.

Hayloft was put in a motor and whirled rapidly to the police station.

On the way the chief handed him a flask and a cigar.

They chatted over the events of the evening.

Hayloft realized that a new life had opened for him. He was no longer a despised outcast. He had entered the American criminal class.

At the police station the chief showed Hezekiah to his room.

"I hope you will like this room," he said a little anxiously. "It is the best that I can give you to-night. To-morrow I can give you a room with a bath, but at such short notice I am sure you will not mind putting up with this."

He said good night and shut the door. In a moment he reappeared.

"About breakfast?" he said. "Would you rather have it in your room, or will you join us at our table d'hôte? The force are most anxious to meet you."

Next morning, before Hezekiah was up, the chief brought to his room a new outfit of clothes—a silk hat, frock-coat, shepherd's-plaid trousers and varnished boots with spats.

"You won't mind accepting these things, Mr. Hayloft. Our force would like very much to enable you to make a suitable appearance in the court."

Carefully dressed and shaved, Hezekiah descended. He was introduced to the leading officials of the force, and spent a pleasant hour of chat over a cigar, discussing the incidents of the night before.

In the course of the morning a number of persons called to meet and congratulate Hezekiah.

"I want to tell you, sir," said the editor of a great American daily, "that your work of last night will be known and commented on all over the States. Your shooting of the footman was a splendid piece of nerve, sir, and will do much in defence of the unwritten law."

"Mr. Hayloft," said another caller, "I am sorry not to have met you sooner. Our friends here tell me that you have been in New York for some months. I regret, sir, that we did not know you. This is the name of my firm, Mr. Hayloft. We are leading lawyers here, and we want the honour of defending you. We may! Thank you, sir. And now, as we have still an hour or two before the court, I want to run you up to my house in my motor. My wife is very anxious to have a little luncheon for you."

The court met that afternoon. There was a cheer as Hezekiah entered.

"Mr. Hayloft," said the judge, "I am adjourning this court for a few days. From what I hear the nerve strain that you have undergone must have been most severe. Your friends tell me that you can hardly be in a state to take a proper interest in the case till you have had a thorough rest."

As Hayloft left the court a cheer went up from the crowd, in which the judge joined.

The next few days were busy days for Hezekiah. Filled with receptions, civic committees, and the preparation of the brief, in which Hezekiah's native intelligence excited the admiration of the lawyers.

Newspaper men sought for interviews. Business promoters called upon Hezekiah. His name was put down as a director of several leading companies, and it was rumoured that in the event of his acquittal he would undertake a merger of all the great burglar protection corporations of the United States.

The trial opened a week later, and lasted two months. Hezekiah was indicted on five charges—arson, for having burned the steel cage of the elevator; misdemeanour, for shooting the footman; the theft of the money, petty larceny; the killing of the philanthropist, infanticide; and the shooting at the police without hitting them, aggravated felony.

The proceedings were very complicated—expert evidence was taken from all over the United States. An analytical examination was made of the brain of the philanthropist. Nothing was found.

The entire jury were dismissed three times on the grounds of prejudice, twice on the ground of ignorance, and finally disbanded on the ground of insanity.

The proceedings dragged on.

Meantime Hezekiah's business interests accumulated.

At length, at Hezekiah's own suggestion, it was necessary to abandon the case.

"Gentlemen," he said, in his final speech to the court, "I feel that I owe an apology for not being able to attend these proceedings any further. At any time, when I can snatch an hour or two from my business, you may always count on my attendance. In the meantime, rest assured that I shall follow your proceedings with the greatest interest."

He left the room amid three cheers and the singing of "Auld Lang Syne."

After that the case dragged hopelessly on from stage to stage.

The charge of arson was met by a *nolle prosequi.* The accusation of theft was stopped by a *ne plus ultra.* The killing of the footman was pronounced justifiable insanity.

The accusation of murder for the death of the philanthropist was withdrawn by common consent. Damages in error were awarded to Hayloft for the loss of his revolver and cartridges. The main body of the case was carried on a writ of *certiorari* to the Federal Courts and appealed to the Supreme Court of the United States.

It is there still.

Meantime, Hezekiah, as managing director of the Burglars' Security Corporation, remains one of the rising generation of financiers in New York, with every prospect of election to the State Senate.

VI

SORROWS OF A SUPER SOUL:
or, The Memoirs of Marie Mushenough

(Translated, by Machinery, out of the Original Russian.)

DO YOU ever look at your face in the glass?
I do.

Sometimes I stand for hours and peer at my face and wonder at it. At times I turn it upside down and gaze intently at it. I try to think what it means. It seems to look back at me with its great brown eyes as if it knew me and wanted to speak to me.

Why was I born?
I do not know.

I ask my face a thousand times a day and find no answer.

At times when people pass my room—my maid Nitnitzka, or Jakub, the serving-man—and see me talking to my face, they think I am foolish.

But I am not.

At times I cast myself on the sofa and bury my head in the cushions. Even then I cannot find out why I was born.

I am seventeen.

Shall I ever be seventy-seven? Ah!

Shall I ever be even sixty-seven, or sixty-seven even? Oh!

And if I am both of these, shall I ever be eight-seven?

I cannot tell.

Often I start up in the night with wild eyes and wonder if I shall be eighty-seven.

Next Day.

I passed a flower in my walk to-day. It grew in the meadow beside the river bank.

It stood dreaming on a long stem.

I knew its name. It was a Tchupvskja. I love beautiful names.

I leaned over and spoke to it. I asked it if my heart would ever know love. It said it thought so.

On the way home I passed an onion.

It lay upon the road.

Someone had stepped upon its stem and crushed it. How it must have suffered. I placed it in my bosom. All night it lay beside my pillow.

Another Day.

My heart is yearning for love! How is it that I can love no one?

I have tried and I cannot. My father—Ivan Ivanovitch—he is so big and so kind, and yet I cannot love him; and my mother, Katoosha Katooshavitch, she is just as big, and yet I cannot love her. And my brother, Dimitri Dimitrivitch, I cannot love him.

And Alexis Alexovitch!

I cannot love him. And yet I am to marry him. They have set the day. It is a month from to-day. One month. Thirty days. Why cannot I love Alexis? He is tall and strong. He is a soldier. He is in the Guard of the Czar, Nicolas Romanoff, and yet I cannot love him.

Next Day but one.

How they cramp and confine me here—Ivan Ivanovitch my father, and my mother (I forget her name for the minute), and all the rest.

I cannot breathe.

They will not let me.

Every time I try to commit suicide they hinder me.

Last night I tried again.

I placed a phial of sulphuric acid on the table beside my bed.

In the morning it was still there.

It had not killed me.

They have forbidden me to drown myself.

Why!

I do not know why? In vain I ask the air and the trees why I should not drown myself? They do not see any reason why.

And yet I long to be free, free as the young birds, as the very youngest of them.

I watch the leaves blowing in the wind and I want to be a leaf.

Yet here they want to make me eat!

Yesterday I ate a banana! Ugh!

Next Day.

To-day in my walk I found a cabbage.

It lay in a corner of the hedge. Cruel boys had chased it there with stones.

It was dead when I lifted it up.

Beside it was an egg.

It too was dead. Ah, how I wept—

This Morning.

How my heart beats. To-day A MAN passed. He passed: actually passed.

From my window I saw him go by the garden gate and out into the meadow beside the river where my Tchupvskja flower is growing!

How beautiful he looked! Not tall like Alexis Alexovitch, ah, no! but so short and wide and round—shaped like the beautiful cabbage that died last week.

He wore a velvet jacket and he carried a camp stool and an easel on his back, and in his face was a curved pipe with a long stem, and his face was not red and rough like the face of Alexis, but mild and beautiful and with a smile that played on it like moonlight over putty.

Do I love him? I cannot tell. Not yet. Love is a gentle plant. You cannot force its growth.

As he passed I leaned from the window and threw a rosebud at him.

But he did not see it.

Then I threw a cake of soap and a toothbrush at him. But I missed him, and he passed on.

Another Day.

Love has come into my life. It fills it. I have seen HIM again. I have spoken with him. He sat beside the river on his camp stool. How beautiful he looked, sitting on it: how strong he seemed and how frail the little stool on which he sat.

Before him was the easel and he was painting. I spoke to him.

I know his name now.

His name—. How my heart beats as I write it—no, I cannot write it, I will whisper it—it is Otto Dinkelspiel.

Is it not a beautiful name? Ah!

He was painting on a canvas—beautiful colours, red and gold and white, in glorious opalescent streaks in all directions.

I looked at it in wonder.

Instinctively I spoke to him. "What are you painting?" I said. "Is it the Heavenly Child?"

"No," he said, "it is a cow!"

Then I looked again and I could see that it was a cow.

I looked straight into his eyes.

"It shall be our secret," I said; "no one else shall know."

And I knew that I loved him.

A Week Later.

Each morning I go to see Otto beside the river in the meadow.

He sits and paints, and I sit with my hands clasped about my knees and talk to him. I tell him all that I think, all that I read, all that I know, all that I feel, all that I do not feel.

He listens to me with that far-away look that I have learned to love and that means that he is thinking deeply; at times he almost seems not to hear.

The intercourse of our minds is wonderful.

We stimulate one another's thought.

Otto is my master. I am his disciple!

Yesterday I asked him if Hegel or Schlegel or Whegel gives the truest view of life.

He said he didn't know! My Otto!

To-day.

Otto touched me! He touched me!

How the recollection of it thrills me!

I stood beside him on the river bank, and as we talked the handle of my parasol touched the bottom button of his waistcoat.

It seemed to burn me like fire!

To-morrow I am to bring Otto to see my father.

But to-night I can think of nothing else but that Otto has touched me.

Next Day.

Otto has touched father! He touched him for ten roubles. My father is furious. I cannot tell what it means.

I brought Otto to our home. He spoke with my father, Ivan Ivanovitch. They sat together in the evening. And now my father is angry. He says that Otto wanted to touch him.

Why should he be angry?

But Otto is forbidden the house, and I can see him only in the meadow.

Two Days Later.

To-day Otto asked me for a keepsake.

I offered him one of my hatpins. But he said no. He has taken instead the diamond buckle from my belt.

I read his meaning.

He means that I am to him as a diamond is to lesser natures.

This Morning.

Yesterday Otto asked me for another keepsake. I took a gold rouble from my bag and said that he should break it in half and that each should keep one of the halves.

But Otto said no. I divined his thought. It would violate our love to break the coin.

He is to keep it for both of us. and it is to remain unbroken like our love.

Is it not a sweet thought?

Otto is so thoughtful. He thinks of everything.

To-day he asked me if I had another gold rouble.

Next Day.

To-day I brought Otto another gold rouble.

His eyes shone with love when he saw it.

He has given me for it a bronze kopek. Our love is to be as pure as gold and as strong as bronze.

Is it not beautiful?

Later.

I am so fearful that Alexis Alexovitch may return.

I fear that if he comes Otto might kill him. Otto is so calm, I dread to think of what would happen if he were aroused.

Next Day.

I have told Otto about Alexis. I have told him that Alexis is a soldier, that he is in the Guards of the Czar, and that I am betrothed to him. At first Otto would not listen to me. He feared that his anger might overmaster him. He began folding up his camp-stool.

Then I told him that Alexis would not come for some time yet, and he grew calmer.

I have begged him for my sake not to kill Alexis. He has given me his promise.

Another Day.

Ivan Ivanovitch, my father, has heard from Alexis. He will return in fourteen days. The day after his return I am to marry him.

And meantime I have still fourteen days to love Otto.

My love is perfect. It makes me want to die. Last night I tried again to commit suicide. Why should I live now that I have known a perfect love? I placed a box of cartridges beside my bed. I awoke unharmed. They did not kill me. But I know what it means. It means that Otto and I are to die together. I must tell Otto.

Later.

To-day I told Otto that we must kill ourselves, that our love is so perfect that we have no right to live.

At first he looked so strange.

He suggested that I should kill myself first and that he should starve himself beside my grave.

But I could not accept the sacrifice.

I offered instead to help him to hang himself beside the river.

He is to think it over. If he does not hang himself, he is to shoot himself. I have lent him my father's revolver. How grateful he looked when he took it.

Next Day.

Why does Otto seem to avoid me? Has he some secret sorrow that I cannot share? To-day he moved his camp-stool to the other side of the meadow. He was in the long grass behind an elderberry bush. At first I did not see him. I thought that he had hanged himself. But he said no. He had forgotten to get a rope. He had tried, he said, to shoot himself. But he had missed himself.

Five Days Later.

Otto and I are not to die. We are to live; to live and love one another for ever! We are going away, out into the world together! How happy I am!

Otto and I are to flee together.

When Alexis comes we shall be gone; we shall be far away.

I have said to Otto that I will fly with him, and he has said yes.

I told him that we would go out into the world together;

empty-handed we would fare forth together and defy the world. I said that he should be my knight-errant, my paladin!

Otto said he would be it.

He has consented. But he says we must not fare forth empty-handed. I do not know why he thinks this, but he is firm, and I yield to my lord. He is making all our preparations.

Each morning I bring to the meadow a little bundle of my things and give them to my knight-errant and he takes them to the inn where he is staying.

Last week I brought my jewel-case, and yesterday, at his request, I took my money from the bank and brought it to my paladin. It will be so safe with him.

To-day he said that I shall need some little things to remember my father and mother by when we are gone. So I am to take my father's gold watch while he is asleep. My hero! How thoughtful he is of my happiness.

Next Day.

All is ready. To-morrow I am to meet Otto at the meadow with the watch and the rest of the things.

To-morrow night we are to flee together. I am to go down to the little gate at the foot of the garden, and Otto will be there.

To-day I have wandered about the house and garden and have said good-bye. I have said good-bye to my Tchupvskja flower, and to the birds and the bees.

To-morrow it will be all over.

Next Evening.

How can I write what has happened! My soul is shattered to its depths.

All that I dreaded most has happened. How can I live!

Alexis has come back. He and Otto have fought.

Ah God! it has been terrible.

I stood with Otto in the meadow. I had brought him the watch, and I gave it to him, and all my love and my life with it.

Then, as we stood, I turned and saw Alexis Alexovitch striding towards us through the grass.

How tall and soldierly he looked! And the thought flashed through my mind that if Otto killed him he would be lying there a dead, inanimate thing.

"Go, Otto," I cried, "go, if you stay you will kill him."

Otto looked and saw Alexis coming. He turned one glance at me: his face was full of infinite meaning.

Then, for my sake, he ran. How noble he looked as he ran. Brave heart! he dared not stay and risk the outburst of his anger.

But Alexis overtook him.

Then beside the river-bank they fought. Ah! but it was terrible to see them fight. Is it not awful when men fight together?

I could only stand and wring my hands and look on in agony!

First, Alexis seized Otto by the waistband of his trousers and swung him round and round in the air. I could see Otto's face as he went round: the same mute courage was written on it as when he turned to run. Alexis swung Otto round and round until his waistband broke, and he was thrown into the grass.

That was the first part of the fight.

Then Alexis stood beside Otto and kicked him from behind as he lay in the grass, and they fought like that for some time. That was the second part of the fight. Then came the third and last part. Alexis picked up the easel and smashed the picture over Otto's head. It fastened itself like a collar about his neck. Then Alexis picked Otto up with the picture round his neck and threw him into the stream.

He floated!

My paladin!

He floated!

I could see his upturned face as he floated onwards down the stream, through the meadow! It was full of deep resignation.

Then Alexis Alexovitch came to me and gathered me up in his arms and carried me thus across the meadow—he is so tall and strong—and whispered that he loved me, and that to-morrow he would shield me from the world. He carried me thus to the house in his arms among the grass and flowers; and there was my father, Ivan Ivanovitch, and my mother, Katoosha Katooshavitch. And to-morrow I am to marry Alexis. He had brought back from the inn my jewels and my money, and he gave me again the diamond clasp that Otto had taken from my waist.

How can I bear it? Alexis is to take me to Petersburg, and he has bought a beautiful house in the Prospekt, and I am to live in it with him, and we are to be rich, and I am to be presented at the Court of Nicholas Romanoff and his wife. Ah! Is it not dreadful?

And I can only think of Otto floating down the stream with the easel about his neck. From the little river he will float into the Dnieper, and from the Dnieper into the Bug, and from the Bug he will float down the Volga, and from the Volga into the Caspian Sea. And from the Caspian Sea there is no outlet, and Otto will float round and round it for ever.

Is it not dreadful?

HANNAH OF THE HIGHLANDS:

or, The Laird of Loch Aucherlocherty

> "Sair maun ye greet, but hoot awa!
> There's muckle yet, love isna' a'—
> Nae more ye'll see, howe'er ye whine
> The bonnie breeks of Auld Lang Syne!"

THE SIMPLE WORDS rang out fresh and sweet upon the morning air.

It was Hannah of the Highlands. She was gathering lobsters in the burn that ran through the glen.

The scene about her was typically Highland. Wild hills rose on both sides of the burn to a height of seventy-five feet, covered with a dense Highland forest that stretched a hundred yards in either direction. At the foot of the burn a beautiful Scotch logch lay in the hollow of the hills. Beyond it again, through the gap of the hills, was the sea. Through the Glen, and close beside the burn where Hannah stood, wound the road that rose again to follow the cliffs along the shore.

The tourists in the Highlands will find no more beautiful spot than the Glen of Aucherlocherty.

Nor is there any spot which can more justly claim to be historic ground.

It was here in the glen that Bonnie Prince Charlie had lain and hidden after the defeat of Culloden. Almost in the same spot the great boulder still stands behind which the Bruce had lain hidden after Bannockburn; while behind a number of lesser stones the Covenanters had concealed themselves during the height of the Stuart persecution.

Through the Glen Montrose had passed on his fateful ride to Killiecrankie; while at the lower end of it the rock was still pointed out behind which William Wallace had paused to change his breeches while flying from the wrath of Rob Roy.

Grim memories such as these gave character to the spot.

Indeed, most of the great events of Scotch history had taken place in the Glen, while the little logch had been the scene of some of the most stirring naval combats in the history of the Grampian Hills.

But there was little in the scene which lay so peaceful on this April morning to recall the sanguinary history of the Glen. Its sides at present were covered with a thick growth of gorse, elderberry, egg-plants, and ghillie flower, while the woods about it were loud with the voice of the throstle, the linnet, the magpie, the jackdaw, and other song-birds of the Highlands.

It was a gloriously beautiful Scotch morning. The rain fell softly and quietly, bringing dampness and moisture, and almost a sense of wetness to the soft moss underfoot. Grey mists flew hither and thither, carrying with them an invigorating rawness that had almost a feeling of dampness.

It is the memory of such a morning that draws a tear from the eye of Scotchmen after years of exile. The Scotch heart, reader, can by moved to its depths by the sight of a raindrop or the sound of a wet rag.

And meantime Hannah, the beautiful Highland girl, was singing. The fresh young voice rose high above the rain. Even the birds seemed to pause to listen, and as they listened to the simple words of the Gaelic folk-song, fell off the bough with a thud on the grass.

The Highland girl made a beautiful picture as she stood.

Her bare feet were in the burn, the rippling water of which laved her ankles. The lobsters played about her feet, or clung affectionately to her toes, as if loath to leave the water and be gathered in the folds of her blue apron.

It was a scene to charm the heart of a Burne-Jones, or an Alma Tadema, or of anybody fond of lobsters.

The girl's golden hair flowed widely behind her, gathered in a single braid with a piece of stovepipe wire.

"Will you sell me one of your lobsters?"

Hannah looked up. There, standing in the burn a few yards above her, was the vision of a young man.

The beautiful Highland girl gazed at him fascinated.

He seemed a higher order of being.

He carried a fishing-rod and basket in his hand. He was dressed in a salmon-fishing costume of an English gentleman. Salmon-fishing boots reached to his thighs, while above them he wore a fishing-jacket fastened loosely with a fishing-belt about his waist. He wore a small fishing-cap on his head.

There were no fish in his basket.

He drew near to the Highland girl.

Hannah knew as she looked at him that it must be Ian McWhinus, the new laird.

At sight she loved him.

"Ye're sair welcome," she said, as she handed to the young man the finest of her lobsters.

He put it in his basket.

Then he felt in the pocket of his jacket and brought out a sixpenny-piece.

"You must let me pay for it," he said.

Hannah took the sixpence and held it a moment, flushing with true Highland pride.

"I'll no be selling the fush for money," she said.

Something in the girl's speech went straight to the young man's heart. He handed her half a crown. Whistling lightly, he strode off up the side of the burn. Hannah stood gazing after him spell-bound. She was aroused from her reverie by an angry voice calling her name.

"Hannah, Hannah," cried the voice, "come away ben; are ye daft, lass, that ye stand there keeking at a McWhinus?"

Then Hannah realized what she had done.

She had spoken with a McWhinus, a thing that no McShamus had done for a hundred and fifty years. For nearly two centuries the McShamuses and the McWhinuses, albeit both dwellers in the Glen, had been torn asunder by one of those painful divisions by which the life of the Scotch people is broken into fragments.

It had arisen out of a point of spiritual belief.

It has been six generations agone at a Highland banquet, in the days when the unrestrained temper of the time gave way to wild orgies, during which theological discussions raged with unrestrained fury. Shamus McShamus, an embittered Calvinist, half crazed perhaps with liquor, had maintained that damnation could be achieved only by faith. Whimper McWhinus had held that damnation could be achieved also by good works. Inflamed with drink, McShamus had struck McWhinus across the temple with an oatcake and killed him. McShamus had been brought to trial. Although defended by some of the most skilled lawyers of Aucherlocherty, he had been acquitted. On the very night of his acquittal, Whangus McWhinus, the son of the murdered man, had lain in wait for Shamus McShamus, in the hollow of the Glen road where it rises to the cliff, and had shot him through the bagpipes. Since then the feud had raged with unquenched bitterness for a century and a half.

With each generation the difference between the two families became more acute. They differed on every possible point. They wore different tartans, sat under different ministers, drank different brands of whisky, and upheld different doctrines in regard to eternal punishment.

To add to the feud the McWhinuses had grown rich, while the McShamuses had become poor.

At least once in every generation a McWhinus or a McShamus had been shot, and always at the turn of the Glen road where it rose to the edge of the cliff. Finally, two generations gone, the McWhinuses had been raised to sudden wealth by the discovery of a coal mine on their land. To show their contempt for the McShamuses they had left the Glen to live in America. The McShamuses, to show their contempt for the McWhinuses, had remained in the Glen. The feud was kept alive in their memory.

And now the descendant of the McWhinuses had come back,

and bought out the property of the Laird of Aucherlocherty beside the Glen. Ian McWhinus knew nothing of the feud. Reared in another atmosphere, the traditions of Scotland had no meaning for him. He had entirely degenerated. To him the tartan had become only a piece of coloured cloth. He wore a kilt as a masquerade costume for a Hallowe'en dance, and when it rained he put on a raincoat. He was no longer Scotch. More than that, he had married a beautiful American wife, a talcum-powder blonde with a dough face and the exquisite rotundity of the packing-house district of the Middle-West. Ian McWhinus was her slave. For her sake he had bought the lobster from Hannah. For her sake, too, he had scrutinized closely the beautiful Highland girl, for his wife was anxious to bring back a Scotch housemaid with her to Chicago.

And meantime Hannah, with the rapture of a new love in her heart, followed her father, Oyster McOyster McShamus, to the cottage. Oyster McOyster, even in advancing age, was a fine specimen of Scotch manhood. Ninety-seven years of age, he was approaching the time when many of his countrymen begin to show the ravages of time. But he bore himself straight as a lath, while his tall stature and his native Highland costume accentuated the fine outline of his form. This costume consisted of a black velvet beetle-shell jacket, which extended from the shoulder half-way down the back, and was continued in a short kilt of the tartan of the McShamuses, which extended from the waist half-way to the thigh. The costume reappeared again after an interval in the form of rolled golf stockings, which extended half-way up to the knee, while on his feet a pair of half shoes were buckled half-way up with a Highland clasp. On his head half-way between the ear and the upper superficies of the skull he wore half a Scotch cap, from which a tall rhinoceros feather extended half-way into the air.

A pair of bagpipes were beneath his arm, from which, as he walked, he blew those deep and plaintive sounds which have done much to imprint upon the characters of those who hear them a melancholy and resigned despair.

At the door of the cottage he turned and faced his daughter.

"What said Ian McWhinus to you i' the burnside?" he said fiercely.

" 'Twas nae muckle," said Hannah, and she added, for the truth was ever more to her than her father's wrath, "he gi'ed me saxpence for a fush."

"Siller!" shrieked the Highlander. "Siller from a McWhinus!"

Hannah handed him the sixpence. Oyster McOyster dashed it fiercely on the ground, and picking it up he dashed it with full force against the wall of the cottage. Then, seizing it again, he dashed it angrily into the pocket of his kilt.

They entered the cottage.

Hannah had never seen her father's face so dour as it looked that night.

Their home seemed changed.

Hannah and her mother and father sat down that night in silence to their simple meal of oatmeal porridge and Scotch whisky. In the evening the mother sat to her spinning. Busily she plied her work, for it was a task of love. Her eldest born, Jamie, was away at college at Edinburgh, preparing for the ministry. His graduation day was approaching, and Jamie's mother was spinning him a pair of breeches against the day. The breeches were to be a surprise. Already they were shaping that way. Oyster McShamus sat reading the Old Testament in silence, while Hannah looked into the peat fire and thought of the beautiful young Laird. Only once the Highlander spoke.

"The McWhinus is back," he said, and his glance turned towards the old flint-lock musket on the wall. That night Hannah dreamed of the feud, of the Glen and the burn, of love, of lobsters, and of the Laird of Loch Aucherlocherty. And when she rose in the morning there was a wistful look in her eyes, and there came no song from her throat.

The days passed.

Each day the beautiful Highland girl saw the young Laird, though her father knew it not.

In the mornings she would see him as he came fishing to the

burn. At times he wore his fishing-suit, at other times he had on a knickerbocker suit of shepherd's plaid with a domino pattern *négligé* shirt. For his sake the beautiful Highland girl made herself more beautiful still. Each morning she would twine a Scotch thistle in her hair, and pin a spray of burdock at her heart.

And at times he spoke to her. How Hannah treasured his words. Once, catching sight of her father in the distance, he had asked her who was the old sardine in the petticoats, and the girl had answered gladly that it was her father, for, as a fisherman's daughter, she was proud to have her father mistaken for a sardine.

At another time he had asked her if she was handy about the work of the house. How Hannah's heart had beat at the question. She made up her mind to spin him a pair of breeches like the ones now finishing for her brother Jamie.

And every evening as the sun set Hannah would watch in secret from the window of the cottage waiting for the young Laird to come past in his motor-car, down the Glen road to the sea. Always he would slacken the car at the sharp turn at the top of the cliff. For six generations no McWhinus had passed that spot after nightfall with his life. But Ian McWhinus knew nothing of the feud.

At times Oyster McOyster would see him pass, and standing at the roadside would call down Gaelic curses on his head.

Once, when her father was from home, Hannah had stood on the roadside, and Ian had stopped the machine and had taken her with him in the car for a ride. Hannah, her heart beating with delight, had listened to him as he explained how the car was worked. Had her father known that she had sat thus beside a McWhinus, he would have slain her where she sat.

The tragedy of Hannah's love ran swiftly to its close.

Each day she met the young Laird at the burn.

Each day she gave him the finest of her lobsters. She wore a new thistle every day.

And every night, in secret as her mother slept, she span a new concentric section of his breeches.

And the young Laird, when he went home, said to the talcum

blonde, that the Highland fisher-girl was not half such a damn fool as she seemed.

Then came the fateful afternoon.

He stood beside her at the burn.

"Hannah," he said, as he bent towards her, "I want to take you to America."

Hannah had fallen fainting in his arms.

Ian propped her against a tree, and went home.

An hour later, when Hannah entered her home, her father was standing behind the fireplace. He was staring fixedly into the fire, with the flint-lock musket in his hands. There was the old dour look of the feud upon his face, and there were muttered curses on his lips. His wife Ellen clung to his arm and vainly sought to quiet him.

"Curse him," he muttered, "I'll e'en kill him the night as he passes in his deil machine."

Then Hannah knew that Oyster McShamus had seen her with Ian beside the burn. She turned and fled from the house. Straight up the road she ran towards the manor-house of Aucherlocherty to warn Ian. To save him from her father's wrath, that was her one thought. Night gathered about the Highland girl as she ran. The rain clouds and the gathering storm hung low with fitful lightning overhead. She still ran on. About her was the rolling of the thunder and the angry roaring of the swollen burn. Then the storm broke upon the darkness with all the fury of the Highland gale. The sky was rent with the fierce play of the elements. Yet on Hannah ran. Again and again the lightning hit her, but she ran on still. She fell over the stones, tripped and stumbled in the ruts, butted into the hedges, cannoned off against the stone walls. But she never stopped. She went quicker and quicker. The storm was awful. Lightning, fire, flame, and thunder were all about her. Trees were falling, hurdles were flying, birds were being struck by lightning. Dogs, sheep, and even cattle were hurled through the air.

She reached the manor-house, and stood a moment at the door. The storm had lulled, the rain ceased, and for a brief moment there was quiet. The light was streaming from the windows of the house. Hannah paused. Suddenly her heart misgave her. Her quick ear had caught the sound of a woman's voice within. She approached the window and looked in. Then, as if rooted to the spot, the Highland girl gazed and listened at the pane.

Ian lay upon a sofa. The *négligé* dressing-gown that he wore enhanced the pallid beauty of his face. Beside him sat the talcum-powder blonde. She was feeding him with chocolates. Hannah understood. Ian had trifled with her love. He had bought her lobsters to win her heart, only to cast it aside.

Hannah turned from the window. She plucked the thistle from her throat and flung it on the ground. The, as she turned her eye, she caught sight of the motor standing in the shed.

"The deil machine!" she muttered, while the wild light of Highland frenzy gathered in her eye; then, as she rushed to it and tore the tarpaulin from off it, "Ye'll no be wanting of a mark the night, Oyster McShamus," she cried.

A moment later, the motor, with Hannah at the wheel, was thundering down the road to the Glen. The power was on to the full, and the demented girl clung tight to the steering-gear as the machine rocked and thundered down the descent. The storm was raging again, and the thunder mingled with the roar of the machine as it coursed madly towards the sea. The great eye of the motor blazed in front. The lurid light of it flashed a second on the trees and the burn as it passed, and flashed blinding on the eyes of Oyster as he stood erect on the cliff-side below, musket in hand, and faced the blazing apparition that charged upon him with the old Highland blood surging in his veins.

It was all over in a moment—a blinding flash of lightning, the report of a musket, a great peal of thunder, and the motor bearing the devoted girl hurled headlong over the cliff.

They found her there in the morning. She lay on her side motionless, half buried in the sand, upturned towards the blue Highland sky, serene now after the passing of the storm. Quiet and still she lay. The sea-birds seemed to pause in their flight to look down on her. The little group of Scotch people that had gathered stood and gazed at her with reverential awe. They made no attempt to put her together. It would have been useless. Her gasoline tubes were twisted and bent, her tank burst, her sprockets broken from their sides, and her steering-gear an utter wreck. The motor would never run again.

After a time they roused themselves from their grief and looked about for Hannah. They found her. She lay among the sand and seaweed, her fair hair soaked in gasoline. Then they looked about for Oyster McShamus. Him, too, they found, lying half buried in the grass and soaked in whisky. Then they looked about for Ellen. They found her lying across the door of the cottage half buried in Jamie's breeches.

Then they gathered them up. Life was not extinct. They chafed their hands. They rubbed their feet. They put hot bricks upon their stomachs. They poured hot whisky down their throats. That brought them to.

Of course.

It always does.

They all lived.

But the feud was done for. That was the end of it. Hannah had put it to the bad.

VII

SOAKED IN SEAWEED:

or, Upset in the Ocean

(An Old-fashioned Sea Story.)

IT WAS in August in 1867 that I stepped on board the deck of the *Saucy Sally*, lying in dock at Gravesend, to fill the berth of second mate.

Let me first say a word about myself.

I was a tall, handsome young fellow, squarely and powerfully built, bronzed by the sun and the moon (and even copper-coloured in spots from the effect of the stars), and with a face in which honesty, intelligence, and exceptional brain power were combined with Christianity, simplicity, and modesty.

As I stepped on the deck I could not help a slight feeling of triumph, as I caught sight of my sailor-like features reflected in a tar-barrel that stood beside the mast, while a little later I could scarcely repress a sense of gratification as I noticed them reflected again in a bucket of bilge water.

"Welcome on board, Mr. Blowhard," called out Captain Bilge, stepping out of the binnacle and shaking hands across the taffrail.

I saw before me a fine sailor-like man of from thirty to sixty, clean-shaven, except for an enormous pair of whiskers, a heavy beard, and a thick moustache, powerful in build, and carrying his beam well aft, in a pair of broad duck trousers across the back of which there would have been room to write a history of the British Navy.

Beside him were the first and third mates, both of them being quiet men of poor stature, who looked at Captain Bilge with what seemed to me an apprehensive expression in their eyes.

The vessel was on the eve of departure. Her deck presented that scene of bustle and alacrity dear to the sailor's heart. Men were busy nailing up the masts, hanging the bowsprit over the side, varnishing the lee-scuppers and pouring hot tar down the companion-way.

Captain Bilge, with a megaphone to his lips, kept calling out to the men in his rough sailor fashion:

"Now, then, don't over-exert yourselves, gentlemen. Remember, please, that we have plenty of time. Keep out of the sun as much as you can. Step carefully in the rigging there, Jones; I fear it's just a little high for you. Tut, tut, Williams, don't get yourself so dirty with that tar, you won't look fit to be seen."

I stood leaning over the gaff of the mainsail and thinking—yes, thinking, dear reader, of my mother. I hope that you will think none the less of me for that. Whenever things look dark, I lean up against something and think of mother. If they get positively black, I stand on one leg and think of father. After that I can face anything.

Did I think, too, of another, younger than mother and fairer than father? Yes, I did. "Bear up, darling," I had whispered as she nestled her head beneath my oilskins and kicked out backward with one heel in the agony of her girlish grief, "in five years the voyage will be over, and after three more like it, I shall come back with money enough to buy a second-hand fishing-net and settle down on shore."

Meantime the ship's preparations were complete. The masts were all in position, the sails nailed up, and men with axes were busily chopping away the gangway.

"All ready?" called the Captain.

"Aye, aye, sir."

"Then hoist the anchor in board and send a man down with the key to open the bar."

Opening the bar! the last sad rite of departure. How often in my voyages have I seen it; the little group of men soon to be exiled from their home, standing about with saddened faces, waiting to see the man with the key open the bar—held there by some strange fascination.

Next morning with a fair wind astern we had buzzed around the corner of England and were running down the Channel.

I know no finer sight, for those who have never seen it, than the English Channel. It is the highway of the world. Ships of all nations are passing up and down, Dutch, Scotch, Venezuelan, and even American.

Chinese junks rush to and fro. Warships, motor yachts, icebergs, and lumber rafts are everywhere. If I add to this fact that so thick a fog hangs over it that it is entirely hidden from sight, my readers can form some idea of the majesty of the scene.

We had now been three days at sea. My first sea-sickness was wearing off, and I thought less of father.

On the third morning Captain Bilge descended to my cabin.

"Mr. Blowhard," he said, "I must ask you to stand double watches."

"What is the matter?" I inquired.

"The two other mates have fallen overboard," he said uneasily, and avoiding my eye.

I contented myself with saying, "Very good, sir," but I could not help thinking it a trifle odd that both the mates should have fallen overboard in the same night.

Surely there was some mystery in this.

Two mornings later the Captain appeared at the breakfast-table with the same shifting and uneasy look in his eye.

"Anything wrong, sir?" I asked.

"Yes," he answered, trying to appear at ease and twisting a fried egg to and fro between his fingers with such nervous force as almost to break it in two—"I regret to say that we have lost the bosun."

"The bosun!" I cried.

"Yes," said Captain Bilge more quietly, "he is overboard. I

blame myself for it, partly. It was early this morning. I was holding him up in my arms to look at an iceberg, and, quite accidentally I assure you—I dropped him overboard."

"Captain Bilge," I asked, "have you taken any steps to recover him?"

"Not as yet," he replied uneasily.

I looked at him fixedly, but said nothing.

Ten days passed.

The mystery thickened. On Thursday two men of the starboard watch were reported missing. On Friday the carpenter's assistant disappeared. On the night of Saturday a circumstance occurred which, slight as it was, gave me some clue as to what was happening.

As I stood at the wheel about midnight, I saw the Captain approach in the darkness carrying the cabin-boy by the hind leg. The lad was a bright little fellow, whose merry disposition had already endeared him to me, and I watched with some interest to see what the Captain would do to him. Arrived at the stern of the vessel, Captain Bilge looked cautiously around a moment and then dropped the boy into the sea. For a brief instant the lad's head appeared in the phosphorus of the waves. The Captain threw a boot at him, sighed deeply, and went below.

Here then was the key to the mystery! The Captain was throwing the crew overboard. Next morning we met at breakfast as usual.

"Poor little Williams has fallen overboard," said the Captain, seizing a strip of ship's bacon and tearing at it with his teeth as if he almost meant to eat it.

"Captain," I said, greatly excited, stabbing at a ship's loaf in my agitation with such ferocity as almost to drive my knife into it—"You threw that boy overboard!"

"I did," said Captain Bilge, grown suddenly quiet, "I threw them all over and intend to throw the rest. Listen Blowhard, you are young, ambitious, and trustworthy. I will confide in you."

Perfectly calm now, he stepped to a locker, rummaged in it a moment, and drew out a faded piece of yellow parchment, which he spread on the table. It was a map or chart. In the centre of it was a circle. In the middle of the circle was a small dot and a letter T, while at one side of the map was a letter N, and against it on the other side a letter S.

"What is this?" I asked.

"Can you not guess?" queried Captain Bilge. "It is a desert island."

"Ah!" I rejoiced with a sudden flash of intuition, "and N is for North and S if for South."

"Blowhard," said the Captain, striking the table with such force as to cause a loaf of ship's bread to bounce up and down three or four times, "you've struck it. That part of it had not yet occurred to me."

"And the letter T?" I asked.

"The treasure, the buried treasure," said the Captain, and turning the map over he read from the back of it—"The point T indicates the spot where the treasure is buried under the sand; it consists of half a million Spanish dollars, and is buried in a brown leather dress-suit case."

"And where is the island?" I inquired, mad with excitement.

"That I do not know," said the Captain. "I intend to sail up and down the parallels of latitude until I find it."

"And meantime?"

"Meantime, the first thing to do is to reduce the number of the crew so as to have fewer hands to divide among. Come, come," he added in a burst of frankness which made me love the man in spite of his shortcomings, "will you join me in this? We'll throw them all over, keeping the cook to the last, dig up the treasure, and be rich for the rest of our lives."

Reader, do you blame me if I said yes? I was young, ardent, ambitious, full of bright hopes and boyish enthusiasm.

"Captain Bilge," I said, putting my hand in his, "I am yours."

"Good," he said, "now go forward to the forecastle and get an idea what the men are thinking."

I went forward to the men's quarters—a plain room in the front of the ship, with only a rough carpet on the floor, a few simple armchairs, writing-desks, spittoons of a plain pattern, and small brass beds with blue-and-green screens. It was Sunday morning, and the men were mostly sitting about in their dressing-gowns.

They rose as I entered and curtseyed.

"Sir," said Tompkins, the bosun's mate, "I think it my duty to tell you that there is a great deal of dissatisfaction among the men."

Several of the men nodded.

"They don't like the way the men keep going overboard," he continued, his voice rising to a tone of uncontrolled passion. "It is positively absurd, sir, and if you will allow me to say so, the men are far from pleased."

"Tompkins," I said sternly, "you must understand that my position will not allow me to listen to mutinous language of this sort."

I returned to the Captain. "I think the men mean mutiny," I said.

"Good," said Captain Bilge, rubbing his hands, "that will get rid of a lot of them, and of course," he added musingly, looking out of the broad old-fashioned port-hole at the stern of the cabin, at the heaving waves of the South Atlantic, "I am expecting pirates at any time, and that will take out quite a few of them. However"—and here he pressed the bell for a cabin-boy—"kindly ask Mr. Tompkins to step this way."

"Tompkins," said the Captain as the bosun's mate entered, "be good enough to stand on the locker and stick your head through the stern port-hole, and tell me what you think of the weather."

"Aye, aye, sir," replied the tar with a simplicity which caused us to exchange a quiet smile.

Tompkins stood on the locker and put his head and shoulders out of the port.

Taking a leg each we pushed him through. We heard him plump into the sea.

"Tompkins was easy," said Captain Bilge. "Excuse me as I enter his death in the log."

"Yes," he continued presently, "it will be a great help if they mutiny. I suppose they will, sooner or later. It's customary to do so. But I shall take no step to precipitate it until we have first fallen in with pirates. I am expecting them in these latitudes at any time. Meantime, Mr. Blowhard," he said, rising, "if you can continue to drop overboard one or two more each week, I shall feel extremely grateful."

Three days later we rounded the Cape of Good Hope and entered upon the inky waters of the Indian Ocean. Our course lay now in zigzags and, the weather being favourable, we sailed up and down at a furious rate over a sea as calm as glass.

On the fourth day a pirate ship appeared. Reader, I do not know if you have ever seen a pirate ship. The sight was one to appal the stoutest heart. The entire ship was painted black, a black flag hung at the masthead, the sails were black, and on the deck people dressed all in black walked up and down arm-in-arm. The words "Pirate Ship" were painted in white letters on the bow. At the sight of it our crew were visibly cowed. It was a spectacle that would have cowed a dog.

The two ships were brought side by side. They were then lashed tightly together with bag string and binder twine, and a gang plank laid between them. In a moment the pirates swarmed upon our deck, rolling their eyes, gnashing their teeth and filing their nails.

Then the fight began. It lasted two hours—with fifteen minutes off for lunch. It was awful. The men grappled with one another, kicked one another from behind, slapped one another across the face, and in many cases completely lost their temper and tried to bite one another. I noticed one gigantic fellow brandishing a knotted towel, and striking right and left among our men, until Captain Bilge rushed at him and struck him flat across the mouth with a banana skin.

At the end of two hours, by mutual consent, the fight was declared a draw. The points standing at sixty-one and a half against sixty-two.

The ships were unlashed, and with three cheers from each crew, were headed on their way.

"Now, then," said the Captain to me aside, "let us see how many of the crew are sufficiently exhausted to be thrown overboard."

He went below. In a few minutes he reappeared, his face deadly pale. "Blowhard," he said, "the ship is sinking. One of the pirates (sheer accident, of course, I blame no one) has kicked a hole in the side. Let us sound the well."

We put our ear to the ship's well. It sounded like water.

The men were put to the pumps and worked with the frenzied effort which only those who have been drowned in a sinking ship can understand.

At six p.m. the well marked one half an inch of water, at nightfall three-quarters of an inch, and at daybreak, after a night of unremitting toil, seven-eighths of an inch.

By noon of the next day the water had risen to fifteen-sixteenths of an inch, and on the next night the sounding showed thirty-one thirty-seconds of an inch of water in the hold. The situation was desperate. At this rate of increase few, if any, could tell where it would rise to in a few days.

That night the Captain called me to his cabin. He had a book of mathematical tables in front of him, and great sheets of vulgar fractions littered the floor on all sides.

"The ship is bound to sink," he said, "in fact, Blowhard, she is sinking. I can prove it. It may be six months or it may take years, but if she goes on like this, sink she must. There is nothing for it but to abandon her."

That night, in the dead of darkness, while the crew were busy at the pumps, the Captain and I built a raft.

Unobserved we cut down the masts, chopped them into suitable lengths, laid them crosswise in a pile and lashed them tightly together with bootlaces.

Hastily we threw on board a couple of boxes of food and bottles of drinking fluid, a sextant, a chronometer, a gas-meter, a bicycle pump and a few other scientific instruments. Then taking advantage of a roll in the motion of the ship, we launched the raft, lowered ourselves upon a line, and under cover of the heavy dark of a tropical night, we paddled away from the doomed vessel.

The break of day found us a tiny speck on the Indian Ocean. We looked about as big as this (.).

In the morning, after dressing, and shaving as best we could, we opened our box of food and drink.

Then came the awful horror of our situation.

One by one the Captain took from the box the square blue tins of canned beef which it contained. We counted fifty-two in all. Anxiously and with drawn faces we watched until the last can was lifted from the box. A single thought was in our minds. When the end came the Captain stood up on the raft with wild eyes staring at the sky.

"The can-opener!" he shrieked, "just Heaven, the can-opener." He fell prostrate.

Meantime, with trembling hands, I opened the box of bottles. It contained lager beer bottles, each with a patent tin top. One by one I took them out. There were fifty-two in all. As I withdrew the last one and saw the empty box before me, I shrieked out— "The thing! the thing! oh, merciful Heaven! The thing you open them with!"

I fell prostrate upon the Captain.

We awoke to find ourselves still a mere speck upon the ocean. We felt even smaller than before.

Over us was the burnished copper sky of the tropics. The heavy, leaden sea lapped the sides of the raft. All about us was a litter of corn beef cans and lager beer bottles. Our sufferings in the ensuing days were indescribable. We beat and thumped at the cans with our fists. Even at the risk of spoiling the tins for ever we hammered them fiercely against the raft. We stamped on them, bit at them and swore at them. We pulled and clawed at the bottles with our hands, and chipped and knocked them against the cans, regardless even of breaking the glass and ruining the bottles.

It was futile.

Then day after day we sat in moody silence, gnawed with hunger, with nothing to read, nothing to smoke, and practically nothing to talk about.

On the tenth day the Captain broke silence.

"Get ready the lots, Blowhard," he said. "It's got to come to that."

"Yes," I answered drearily, "we're getting thinner every day."

Then, with the awful prospect of cannibalism before us, we drew lots.

I prepared the lots and held them to the Captain. He drew the longer one.

"Which does that mean," he asked, trembling between hope and despair. "Do I win?"

"No, Bilge," I said sadly, "you lose."

But I mustn't dwell on the days that followed—the long quiet days of lazy dreaming on the raft, during which I slowly built up my strength, which had been shattered by privation. They were days, dear reader, of deep and quiet peace, and yet I cannot recall them without shedding a tear for the brave man who made them what they were.

It was on the fifth day after that I was awakened from a sound sleep by the bumping of the raft against the shore. I had eaten perhaps overheartily, and had not observed the vicinity of land.

Before me was an island, the circular shape of which, with its low, sandy shore, recalled at once its identity.

"The treasure island," I cried, "at last I am rewarded for all my heroism."

In a fever of haste I rushed to the centre of the island. What was the sight that confronted me? A great hollow scooped in the sand, an empty dress-suit case lying beside it, and on a ship's plank driven deep into the sand, the legend, "*Saucy Sally*, October, 1867." So! the miscreants had made good the vessel, headed it for the island of whose existence they must have learned from the chart we so carelessly left upon the cabin table, and had plundered poor Bilge and me of our well-earned treasure!

Sick with the sense of human ingratitude I sank upon the sand.

The island became my home.

There I eked out a miserable existence, feeding on sand and gravel and dressing myself in cactus plants. Years passed. Eating sand and mud slowly undermined my robust constitution. I fell ill. I died. I buried myself.

Would that others who write sea stories would do as much.

IX

CAROLINE'S CHRISTMAS:
or, The Inexplicable Infant

IT WAS XMAS—Xmas with its mantle of white snow, scintillating from a thousand diamond points, Xmas with its good cheer, its peace on earth—Xmas with its feasting and merriment, Xmas with its—well, anyway, it was Xmas.

Or no, that's a slight slip; it wasn't exactly Xmas, it was Xmas Eve, Xmas Eve with its mantle of white snow lying beneath the calm moonlight—and, in fact, with practically the above list of accompanying circumstances with a few obvious emendations.

Yes, it was Xmas Eve.

And more than that!

Listen to *where* it was Xmas.

It was Xmas Eve on the Old Homestead. Reader, do you know, by sight, the Old Homestead? In the pauses of your work at your city desk, where you have grown rich and avaricious, does it never rise before your mind's eye, the quiet old homestead that knew you as a boy before your greed of gold tore you away from it? The Old Homestead that stands beside the road just on the rise of the hill, with its dark spruce trees wrapped in snow, the snug barns and straw stacks behind it; while from its windows there streams a shaft of light from a coal-oil lamp, about as thick as a slate pencil that you can see four miles away, from the other side of the cedar swamp in the hollow. Don't talk to me of your modern searchlights and your incandescent arcs, beside that gleam of light from the coal-oil lamp in the farmhouse window. It will shine clear to the heart across thirty years of distance. Do you not turn, I say, sometimes, reader, from the roar and hustle of the city with its ill-gotten wealth and its godless creed of mammon, to think of the quiet homestead under the brow of the hill? You don't! Well, you skunk!

It was Xmas Eve.

The light shone from the windows of the homestead farm. The light of the log fire rose and flickered and mingled its red glare on the windows with the calm yellow of the lamplight.

John Enderby and his wife sat in the kitchen room of the farmstead. Do you know it, reader, the room called the kitchen?—with the open fire on its old brick hearth, and the cook stove in the corner. It is the room of the farm where people cook and eat and live. It is the living-room. The only other room beside the bedroom is the small room in front, chill-cold in winter, with an organ in it for playing "Rock of Ages" on, when company came. But this room is only used for music and funerals. The real room of the old farm is the kitchen. Does it not rise up before you, reader? It doesn't? Well, you darn fool!

At any rate there sat old John Enderby beside the plain deal table, his head bowed upon his hands, his grizzled face with its unshorn stubble stricken down with the lines of devastating trouble. From time to time he rose and cast a fresh stick of tamarack into the fire with a savage thud that sent a shower of sparks up the chimney. Across the fireplace sat his wife Anna on a straight-backed chair, looking into the fire with the mute resignation of her sex.

What was wrong with them anyway? Ah, reader, can you ask? Do you know or remember so little of the life of the old homestead? When I have said that it is the Old Homestead and Xmas Eve, and that the farmer is in great trouble and throwing tamarack at the fire, surely you ought to guess!

The Old Homestead was mortgaged! Ten years ago, reckless with debt, crazed with remorse, mad with despair and persecuted with rheumatism, John Enderby had mortgaged his farmstead for twenty-four dollars and thirty cents.

To-night the mortgage fell due, to-night at midnight, Xmas

night. Such is the way in which mortgages of this kind are always drawn. Yes, sir, it was drawn with such diabolical skill that on this night of all nights the mortgage would be foreclosed. At midnight the men would come with hammer and nails and foreclose it, nail it up tight.

So the afflicted couple sat.

Anna, with the patient resignation of her sex, sat silent or at times endeavoured to read. She had taken down from the little wall-shelf Bunyan's *Holy Living and Holy Dying*. She tried to read it. She could not. Then she had taken Dante's *Inferno*. She could not read it. Then she had selected Kant's *Critique of Pure Reason*. But she could not read it either. Lastly, she had taken the Farmer's Almanac for 1911. The books lay littered about her as she sat in patient despair.

John Enderby showed all the passion of an uncontrolled nature. At times he would reach out for the crock of buttermilk that stood beside him and drained a draught of the maddening liquid, till his brain glowed like the coals of the tamarack fire before him.

"John," pleaded Anna, "leave alone the buttermilk. It only maddens you. No good ever came of that."

"Aye, lass," said the farmer, with a bitter laugh, as he buried his head again in the crock, "what care I if it maddens me."

"Ah, John, you'd better be employed in reading the Good Book than in your wild courses. Here take it, father, and read it"—and she handed to him the well-worn black volume from the shelf. Enderby paused a moment and held the volume in his hand. He and his wife had known nothing of religious teaching in the public schools of their day, but the first-class non-sectarian education that the farmer had received had stood him in good stead.

"Take the book," she said. "Read, John, in this hour of affliction; it brings comfort."

The farmer took from her hand the well-worn copy of Euclid's *Elements*, and laying aside his hat with reverence, he read aloud: "The angles at the base of an isoceles triangle are equal, and whosoever shall produce the sides, lo, the same also shall be equal each unto each."

The farmer put the book aside.

"It's no use, Anna.I can't read the good words to-night."

He rose, staggered to the crock of buttermilk, and before his wife could stay his hand, drained it to the last drop.

Then he sank heavily to his chair.

"Let them foreclose it, if they will," he said; "I am past caring."

The woman looked sadly into the fire.

"Ah, if only her son Henry had been here. Henry, who had left them three years agone, and whose bright letters still brought from time to time the gleam of hope to the stricken farmhouse.

Henry was in Sing Sing. His letters brought news to his mother of his steady success; first in the baseball nine of the prison, a favourite with his wardens and the chaplain, the best bridge player of the corridor. Henry was pushing his way to the front with the oldtime spirit of the Enderbys.

His mother had hoped that he might have been with her at Xmas, but Henry had written that it was practically impossible for him to leave Sing Sing. He could not see his way out. The authorities were arranging a dance and sleighing party for the Xmas celebration. He had some hope, he said, of slipping away unnoticed, but his doing so might excite attention.

Of the trouble at home Anna had told her son nothing.

No, Henry could not come. There was no help there. And William, the other son, ten years older than Henry. Alas, William had gone forth from the old homestead to fight his way in the great city! "Mother," he had said, "when I make a million dollars I'll come home. Till then good-bye," and he had gone.

How Anna's heart had beat for him. Would he make that million dollars? Would she ever live to see it? And as the years passed she and John had often sat in the evenings picturing William at home again, bringing with him a million dollars, or picturing the million dollars sent by express with love. But the years had passed. William came not. He did not come. The great city had swallowed him up as it has many another lad from the old homestead.

Anna started from her musing—

What was that at the door? The sound of a soft and timid

rapping, and through the glass of the door-pane, a face, a woman's face looking into the fire-lit room with pleading eyes. What was it she bore in her arms, the little bundle that she held tight to her breast to shield it from the falling snow? Can you guess, reader? Try three guesses and see. Right you are. That's what it was.

The farmer's wife went hastily to the door.

"Lord's mercy!" she cried, "what are you doing out on such a night? Come in, child, to the fire."

The woman entered, carrying the little bundle with her, and looking with wide eyes (they were at least an inch and a half across) at Enderby and his wife. Anna could see that there was no wedding-ring on her hand.

"Your name?" said the farmer's wife.

"My name is Caroline," the girl whispered. The rest was lost in the low tones of her voice. "I want shelter," she paused, "I want you to take the child."

Anna took the baby and laid it carefully on the top shelf of the cupboard, then she hastened to bring a glass of water and a dough-nut, and set it before the half-frozen girl.

"Eat," she said, "and warm yourself."

John rose from his seat.

"I'll have no child of that sort here," he said.

"John, John," pleaded Anna, "remember what the Good Book says: "Things which are equal to the same thing are equal to one another!""

John sank back to his chair.

And why had Caroline no wedding-ring? Ah, reader, can you not guess. Well, you can't. It wasn't what you think at all; so there. Caroline had no wedding-ring because she had thrown it away in bitterness, as she tramped the streets of the great city. "Why," she cried, "should the wife of a man in the penitentiary wear a ring."

Then she had gone forth with the child from what had been her home.

It was the old sad story.

She had taken the baby and laid it tenderly, gently on a seat in the park. Then she walked rapidly away. A few minutes after a man had chased after Caroline with the little bundle in his arms. "I beg your pardon," he said, panting, "I think you left your baby in the park." Caroline thanked him.

Next she took the baby to the Grand Central Waiting-room, kissed it tenderly, and laid it on a shelf behind the lunch-counter.

A few minutes later an official, beaming with satisfaction, had brought it back to her.

"Yours, I think, madame," he said, as he handed it to her. Caroline thanked him.

Then she had left it at the desk of the Waldorf Astoria, and at the ticket-office of the subway.

It always came back.

Once or twice she took it to Brooklyn Bridge and threw it into the river, but perhaps something in the way it fell through the air touched the mother's heart and smote her, and she had descended to the river and fished it out.

Then Caroline had taken the child to the country. At first she thought to leave it on the wayside and she had put it down in the snow, and standing a little distance off had thrown mullein stalks at it, but something in the way the little bundle lay covered in the snow appealed to the mother's heart.

She picked it up and went on. "Somewhere," she murmured, "I shall find a door of kindness open to it." Soon after she had staggered into the homestead.

Anna, with true woman's kindness, asked no questions. She put the baby carefully away in a trunk, saw Caroline safely to bed in the best room, and returned to her seat beside the fire.

The old clock struck twenty minutes past eight.

Again a knock sounded at the door.

There entered the familiar figure of the village lawyer. His astrachan coat of yellow dogskin, his celluloid collar, and boots which reached no higher than the ankle, contrasted with the rude surroundings of the little room.

"Enderby," he said, "can you pay?"

"Lawyer Perkins," said the farmer, "give me time and I will; so help me, give me five years more and I'll clear this debt to the last cent."

"John," said the lawyer, touched in spite of his rough (dogskin) exterior, "I couldn't, if I would. These things are not what they were. It's a big New York corporation, Pinchem & Company, that makes these loans now, and they take their money on the day, or they sell you up. I can't help it. So there's your notice, John, and I am sorry! No, I'll take no buttermilk, I must keep a clear head to work," and with that he hurried out into the snow again.

John sat brooding in his chair.

The fire flickered down.

The old clock struck half-past eight, then it half struck a quarter to nine, then slowly it struck striking.

Presently Enderby rose, picked a lantern from its hook. "Mortgage or no mortgage," he said, "I must see to the stock."

He passed out of the house, and standing in the yard, looked over the snow to the cedar swamp beyond with the snow winding through it, far in the distance the lights of the village far away.

He thought of the forty years he had spent here on the homestead—the rude, pioneer days—the house he had build for himself, with its plain furniture, the old-fashioned spinning-wheel on which Anna had spun his trousers, the wooden telephone and the rude skidway on which he ate his meals.

He looked out over the swamp and sighed.

Down in the swamp, two miles away, could he but have seen it, there moved a sleigh, and in it a man dressed in a sealskin coat and silk hat, whose face beamed in the moonlight as he turned to and fro and stared at each object by the roadside as at an old familiar scene. Round his waist was a belt containing a million dollars in gold coin, and as he halted his horse in an opening of the road he unstrapped the belt and counted the coins.

Beside him there crouched in the bushes at the dark edge of the swamp road, with eyes that watched every glitter of the coins, and a hand that grasped a heavy cudgel of blackthorn, a man whose close-cropped hair and hard lined face belonged nowhere but within the walls of Sing Sing.

When the sleigh started again the man in the bushes followed doggedly in its track.

Meantime John Enderby had made the rounds of his outbuildings. He bedded the fat cattle that blinked in the flashing light of the lantern. He stood a moment among his hogs, and, farmer as he was, forgot his troubles a moment to speak to each, calling them by name. It smote him to think how at times he had been tempted to sell one of the hogs, or even to sell the cattle to clear the mortgage off the place. Thank God, however, he had put that temptation behind him.

As he reached the house a sleigh was standing on the roadway. Anna met him at the door. "John," she said, "there was a stranger came while you were in the barn, and wanted a lodging for the night; a city man, I reckon, by his clothes. I hated to refuse him, and I put him in Willie's room. We'll never want it again, and he's gone to sleep."

"Ay, we can't refuse."

John Enderby took out the horse to the barn, and then returned to his vigil with Anna beside the fire.

The fumes of the buttermilk had died out of his brain. He was thinking, as he sat there, of midnight and what it would bring.

In the room above, the man in the sealskin coat had thrown himself down, clothes and all, upon the bed, tired with his drive.

"How it all comes back to me," he muttered as he fell asleep, "the same old room, nothing changed—except them—how worn they look," and a tear started to his eyes. He thought of his leaving his home fifteen years ago, of his struggle in the great city, of the great idea he had conceived of making money, and of the Farm Investment Company he had instituted—the simple system of applying the crushing power of capital to exact the uttermost penny from the farm loans. And now here he was back again, true to his word, with a million dollars in his belt. "To-morrow," he had murmured, "I will tell them. It will be Xmas." Then William—yes, reader, it was William (see line 503 above) had fallen asleep.

The hours passed, and kept passing.

It was 11.30.

Then suddenly Anna started from her place.

"Henry!" she cried as the door opened and a man entered. He advanced gladly to meet her, and in a moment mother and son were folded in a close embrace. It was Henry, the man from Sing Sing. True to his word, he had slipped away unostentatiously at the height of the festivities.

"Alas, Henry," said the mother after the warmth of the first greetings had passed, "you come at an unlucky hour." They told him of the mortgage on the farm and the ruin of his home.

"Yes," said Anna, "not even a bed to offer you," and she spoke of the strangers who had arrived; of the stricken woman and the child, and the rich man in the sealskin coat who had asked for a night's shelter.

Henry listened intently while they told him of the man, and a sudden light of intelligence flashed into his eye.

"By Heaven, father, I have it!" he cried. Then dropping his voice, he said, "Speak low, father. This man upstairs, he had a sealskin coat and silk hat?"

"Yes," said the father.

"Father," said Henry, "I saw a man sitting in a sleigh in the cedar swamp. He had money in his hand, and he counted it, and chuckled,—five dollar gold pieces—in all, 1,125,465 dollars and a quarter."

The father and son looked at one another.

"I see your idea," said Enderby sternly.

"We'll choke him," said Henry.

"Or club him," said the farmer, "and pay the mortgage."

Anna looked from one to the other, joy and hope struggling with the sorrow in her face. "Henry, my Henry," she said proudly, "I knew he would find a way."

"Come on," said Henry; "bring the lamp, mother, take the club, father," and gaily, but with hushed voices, the three stole up the stairs.

The stranger lay sunk in sleep. The back of his head was turned to them as they came in.

"Now, mother," said the farmer firmly, "hold the lamp a little nearer; just behind the ear, I think, Henry."

"No," said Henry, rolling back his sleeve and speaking with the quick authority that sat well upon him, "across the jaw, father, it's quicker and neater."

"Well, well," said the farmer, smiling proudly, "have your own way, lad, you know best."

Henry raised the club.

But as he did so—stay, what was that? Far away behind the cedar swamp the deep booming of the bell of the village church began to strike out midnight. One, two, three, its tones came clear across the crisp air. Almost at the same moment the clock below began with deep strokes to mark the midnight hour; from the farmyard chicken coop a rooster began to crow twelve times, while the loud lowing of the cattle and the soft cooing of the hogs seemed to usher in the morning of Christmas with its message of peace and goodwill.

The club fell from Henry's hand and rattled on the floor.

The sleeper woke, and sat up.

"Father! Mother!" he cried.

"My son, my son," sobbed the father, "we had guessed it was you. We had come to wake you."

"Yes, it is I," said William, smiling to his parents, "and I have brought the million dollars. Here it is," and with that he unstrapped the belt from his waist and laid a million dollars on the table.

"Thank Heaven!" cried Anna, "our troubles are at an end. This money will help clear the mortgage—and the greed of Pinchem & Co. cannot harm us now."

"The farm was mortgaged!" said William, aghast.

"Ay," said the farmer, "mortgaged to men who have no

conscience, whose greedy hand has nearly brought us to the grave. See how she has aged, my boy," and he pointed to Anna.

"Father," said William, in deep tones of contrition, "I am Pinchem & Co. Heaven help me! I see it now. I see at what expense of suffering my fortune was made. I will restore it all, these million dollars, to those I have wronged."

"No," said his mother softly. "You repent, dear son, with true Christian repentance. That is enough. You may keep the money. We will look upon it as a trust, a sacred trust, and every time we spend a dollar of it on ourselves we will think of it as a trust."

"Yes," said the farmer softly, "your mother is right, the money is a trust, and we will restock the farm with it, buy out the Jones's property, and regard the whole thing as a trust."

At this moment the door of the room opened. A woman's form appeared. It was Caroline, robed in one of Anna's directoire nightgowns.

"I heard your voices," she said, and then, as she caught sight of Henry, she gave a great cry.

"My husband!"

"My wife," said Henry, and folded her to his heart.

"You have left Sing Sing?" cried Caroline with joy.

"Yes, Caroline," said Henry. "I shall never go back."

Gaily the reunited family descended. Anna carried the lamp, Henry carried the club. William carried the million dollars.

The tamarack fire roared again upon the hearth. The buttermilk circulated from hand to hand. William and Henry told and retold the story of their adventures. The first streak of the Christmas morn fell through the doorpane.

"Ah, my sons," said John Enderby, "henceforth let us stick to the narrow path. What is it that the Good Book says: 'A straight line is that which lies evenly between its extreme points.'"

X

THE MAN IN ASBESTOS:
An Allegory of the Future

TO BEGIN WITH let me admit that I did it on purpose. Perhaps it was partly from jealousy.

It seemed unfair that other writers should be able at will to drop into a sleep of four or five hundred years, and to plunge headfirst into a distant future and be a witness of its marvels.

I wanted to do that too.

I always had been, I still am, a passionate student of social problems. The world of today with its roaring machinery, the unceasing toil of its working classes, its strife, its poverty, its war, its cruelty, appals me as I look at it. I love to think of the time that must come some day when man will have conquered nature, and the toil-worn human race enter upon an era of peace.

I loved to think of it, and I longed to see it.

So I set about the thing deliberately.

What I wanted to do was to fall asleep after the customary fashion, for two or three hundred years at least, and wake and find myself in the marvel world of the future.

I made my preparations for the sleep.

I bought all the comic papers that I could find, even the illustrated ones. I carried them up to my room in my hotel: with them I brought up a pork pie and dozens and dozens of doughnuts. I ate the pie and the doughnuts, then sat back in the bed and read the comic papers one after the other. Finally, as I felt the awful lethargy stealing upon me, I reached out my hand for the *London Weekly Times*, and held up the editorial page before my eye.

It was, in a way, clear, straight suicide, but I did it.

I could feel my senses leaving me. In the room across the hall there was a man singing. His voice, that had been loud, came fainter and fainter through the transom. I fell into a sleep, the deep immeasurable sleep in which the very existence of the outer world was hushed. Dimly I could feel the days go past, then the years, and then the long passage of the centuries.

Then, not as it were gradually, but quite suddenly, I woke up, sat up, and looked about me.

Where was I?

Well might I ask myself.

I found myself lying, or rather sitting up, on a broad couch. I was in a great room, dim, gloomy, and dilapidated in its general appearance, and apparently, from its glass cases and the stuffed figures that they contained, some kind of museum.

Beside me sat a man. His face was hairless, but neither old nor young. He wore clothes that looked like the grey ashes of paper that had burned and kept its shape. He was looking at me quietly, but with no particular surprise or interest.

"Quick," I said, eager to begin; "where am I? Who are you? What year is this; is it the year 3000, or what is it?"

He drew in his breath with a look of annoyance on his face.

"What a queer, excited way you have of speaking," he said.

"Tell me," I said again, "is this the year 3000?"

"I think I know what you mean," he said; "but really I haven't the faintest idea. I should think it must be at least that, within a hundred years or so; but nobody has kept track of them for so long, it's hard to say."

"Don't you keep track of them any more?" I gasped.

"We used to," said the man. "I myself can remember that a century or two ago there were still a number of people who used to try to keep track of the year, but it died out along with so many other faddish things of that kind. Why," he continued, showing for the first time a sort of animation in his talk, "what was the use of it? You see, after we eliminated death——"

"Eliminated death!" I cried, sitting upright. "Good God!"

"What was that expression you used?" queried the man.

"Good God!" I repeated.

"Ah," he said, "never heard it before. But I was saying that after we had eliminated Death, and Food, and Change, we had practically got rid of Events, and——"

"Stop!" I said, my brain reeling. "Tell me one thing at a time."

"Humph!" he ejaculated. "I see, you must have been asleep a long time. Go on then and ask questions. Only, if you don't mind, just as few as possible, and please don't get interested or excited."

Oddly enough the first question that sprang to my lips was—

"What are those clothes made of?"

"Asbestos," answered the man. "They last hundreds of years. We have one suit each, and there are billions of them piled up, if anybody wants a new one."

"Thank you," I answered. "Now tell me where I am?"

"You are in a museum. The figures in the cases are specimens like yourself. But here," he said, "if you want really to find out about what is evidently a new epoch to you, get off your platform and come out on Broadway and sit on a bench."

I got down.

As we passed through the dim and dust-covered buildings I looked curiously at the figures in the cases.

"By Jove!" I said, looking at one figure in blue clothes with a belt and baton, "that's a policeman!"

"Really," said my new acquaintance, "is *that* what a *policeman* was? I've often wondered. What used they to be used for?"

"Used for?" I repeated in perplexity. "Why, they stood at the corner of the street."

"Ah, yes, I see," he said, "so as to shoot at the people. You must excuse my ignorance," he continued, "as to some of your social customs in the past. When I took my education I was operated upon for social history, but the stuff they used was very inferior."

I didn't in the least understand what the man meant, but had no time to question him, for at that moment we came out upon the street, and I stood riveted in astonishment.

Broadway! Was it possible? The change was absolutely

appalling! In place of the roaring thoroughfare that I had known, this silent, moss-grown desolation. Great buildings fallen into ruin through the sheer stress of centuries of wind and weather, the sides of them coated over with a growth of fungus and moss! The place was soundless. Not a vehicle moved. There were no wires overhead—no sound of life or movement except, here and there, there passed slowly to and fro human figures dressed in the same asbestos clothes as my acquaintance, with the same hairless faces, and the same look of infinite age upon them.

Good heavens! And was this the era of the Conquest that I had hoped to see! I had always taken for granted, I do not know why, that humanity was destined to move forward. This picture of what seemed desolation on the ruins of our civilization rendered me almost speechless.

There were little benches placed here and there on the street. We sat down.

"Improved, isn't it," said the man in asbestos, "since the days when you remember it?"

He seemed to speak quite proudly.

I gasped out a question.

"Where are the street cars and the motors?"

"Oh, done away with long ago," he said; "how awful they must have been. The noise of them!" and his asbestos clothes rustled with a shudder.

"But how do you get about?"

"We don't," he answered. "Why should we? It's just the same being here as being anywhere else." He looked at me with an infinity of dreariness in his face.

A thousand questions surged into my mind at once. I asked one of the simplest.

"But how do you get back and forwards to your work?"

"Work!" he said. "There isn't any work. It's finished. The last of it was all done centuries ago."

I looked at him a moment open-mouthed. Then I turned and looked again at the grey desolation of the street with the asbestos figures moving here and there.

I tried to pull my senses together. I realized that if I was to unravel this new and undreamed-of future, I must go at it systematically and step by step.

"I see," I said after a pause, "that momentous things have happened since my time. I wish you would let me ask you about it all systematically, and would explain it to me bit by bit. First, what do you mean by saying that there is no work?"

"Why," answered my strange acquaintance, "it died out of itself. Machinery killed it. If I remember rightly, you had a certain amount of machinery even in your time. You had done very well with steam, made a good beginning with electricity, though I think radial energy had hardly as yet been put to use."

I nodded assent.

"But you found it did you no good. The better your machines, the harder you worked. The more things you had the more you wanted. The pace of life grew swifter and swifter. You cried out, but it would not stop. You were all caught in the cogs of your own machine. None of you could see the end."

"That is quite true," I said. "How do you know it all?"

"Oh," answered the Man in Asbestos, "that part of my education was very well operated—I see you do not know what I mean. Never mind, I can tell you that later. Well, then, there came, probably almost two hundred years after your time, the Era of the Great Conquest of Nature, the final victory of Man and Machinery."

"They did conquer it?" I asked quickly, with a thrill of the old hope in my veins again.

"Conquered it," he said, "beat it out! Fought it to a standstill! Things came one by one, then faster and faster, in a hundred years it was all done. In fact, just as soon as mankind turned its energy to decreasing its needs instead of increasing its desires, the whole thing was easy. Chemical Food came first. Heavens! the simplicity of it. And in your time thousands of millions of people tilled and grubbed at the soil from morning till night. I've seen specimens of them—farmers, they called them. There's one in the museum. After the invention of Chemical Food we piled up enough in the emporiums in a year to last for centuries. Agriculture went overboard. Eating and all that goes with it, domestic labour, housework—all ended. Nowadays one takes a concentrated pill every year or so, that's all. The whole digestive apparatus, as you knew it, was a clumsy thing that had been bloated up like a set of bagpipes through the evolution of its use!"

I could not forbear to interrupt. "Have you and these people," I said, "no stomachs—no apparatus?"

"Of course we have," he answered, "but we use it to some purpose. Mine is largely filled with my education—but there! I am anticipating again. Better let me go on as I was. Chemical Food came first: that cut off almost one-third of the work, and then came Asbestos Clothes. That was wonderful! In one year humanity made enough suits to last for ever and ever. That, of course, could never have been if it hadn't been connected with the revolt of women and the fall of Fashion."

"Have the Fashions gone," I asked, "that insane, extravagant idea of——" I was about to launch into one of my old-time harangues about the sheer vanity of decorative dress, when my eye rested on the moving figures in asbestos, and I stopped.

"All gone," said the Man in Asbestos. "Then next to that we killed, or practically killed, the changes of climate. I don't think that in your day you properly understood how much of your work was due to the shifts of what you called the weather. It meant the need of all kinds of special clothes and houses and shelters, a wilderness of work. How dreadful it must have been in your day—wind and storms, great wet masses—what did you call them?—clouds—flying through the air, the ocean full of salt, was it not?—tossed and torn by the wind, snow thrown all over everything, hail, rain—how awful!"

"Sometimes," I said, "it was very beautiful. But how did you alter it?"

"Killed the weather!" answered the Man in Asbestos. "Simple as anything—turned its forces loose one against the other, altered the composition of the sea so that the top became all more or less gelatinous. I really can't explain it, as it is an operation that I never took at school, but it made the sky grey, as you see it, and the sea gum-coloured, the weather all the same. It cut out fuel and houses and an infinity of work with them!"

He paused a moment. I began to realize something of the course of evolution that had happened.

"So," I said, "the conquest of nature meant that presently there was no more work to do?"

"Exactly," he said, "nothing left."

"Food enough for all?"

"Too much," he answered.

"Houses and clothes?"

"All you like," said the Man in Asbestos, waving his hand. "There they are. Go out and take them. Of course, they're falling down—slowly, very slowly. But they'll last for centuries yet, nobody need bother."

Then I realized, I think for the first time, just what work had meant in the old life, and how much of the texture of life itself had been bound up in the keen effort of it.

Presently my eyes looked upward: dangling at the top of a moss-grown building I saw what seemed to be the remains of telephone wires.

"What became of all that," I said, "the telegraph and the telephone and all the system of communication?"

"Ah," said the Man in Asbestos, "that was what a telephone meant, was it? I knew that it had been suppressed centuries ago. Just what was it for?"

"Why," I said with enthusiasm, "by means of the telephone we could talk to anybody, call up anybody, and talk at any distance."

"And anybody could call you up at any time and talk?" said the Man in Asbestos, with something like horror. "How awful! What a dreadful age yours was, to be sure. No, the telephone and all the rest of it, all the transportation and intercommunication was cut out and forbidden. There was no sense in it. You see," he added, "what you don't realize is that people after your day became gradually more and more reasonable. Take the railroad, what good was that? It brought into every town a lot of people from every other town. Who wanted them? Nobody. When work stopped and commerce ended, and food was needless, and the weather killed, it was foolish to move about. So it was all terminated. Anyway," he said, with a quick look of apprehension and a change in his voice, "it was dangerous!"

"So!" I said. "Dangerous! You still have danger?"

"Why, yes," he said, "there's always the danger of getting broken."

"What do you mean," I asked.

"Why," said the Man in Asbestos, "I suppose it's what you would call being dead. Of course, in one sense there's been no death for centuries past; we cut that out. Disease and death were simply a matter of germs. We found them one by one. I think that even in your day you had found one or two of the easier, the bigger ones?"

I nodded.

"Yes, you had found diphtheria and typhoid and, if I am right, there were some outstanding, like scarlet fever and smallpox, that you called ultra-microscopic, and which you were still hunting for, and others that you didn't even suspect. Well, we hunted them down one by one and destroyed them. Strange that it never occurred to any of you that Old Age was only a germ! It turned out to be quite a simple one, but it was so distributed in its action that you never even thought of it."

"And you mean to say," I ejaculated in amazement, looking at the Man in Asbestos, "that nowadays you live for ever?"

"I wish," he said, "that you hadn't that peculiar, excitable way of talking; you speak as if everything *mattered* so tremendously. Yes," he continued, "we live for ever, unless, of course, we get broken. That happens sometimes. I mean that we may fall over a high place or bump on something, and snap ourselves. You see, we're just a little brittle still,—some remnant, I suppose, of the Old Age germ—and we have to be careful. In fact," he continued, "I don't mind saying that accidents of this sort were the most distressing feature of our civilization till we took steps to cut out all accidents. We forbid all street cars, street traffic, aeroplanes, and so on. The risks of your time," he said, with a shiver of his asbestos clothes, "must have been awful."

"They were," I answered, with a new kind of pride in my generation that I had never felt before, "but we thought it part of the duty of brave people to——"

"Yes, yes," said the Man in Asbestos impatiently, "please don't get excited. I know what you mean. It was quite irrational."

We sat silent for a long time. I looked about me at the crumbling buildings, the monotone, unchanging sky, and the dreary, empty street. Here, then, was the fruit of the Conquest, here was the elimination of work, the end of hunger and of cold, the cessation of the hard struggle, the downfall of change and death—nay, the very millennium of happiness. And yet, somehow, there seemed something wrong with it all. I pondered, then I put two or three rapid questions, hardly waiting to reflect upon the answers.

"Is there any war now?"

"Done with centuries ago. They took to settling international disputes with a slot machine. After that all foreign dealings were given up. Why have them? Everybody thinks foreigners awful."

"Are there any newspapers now?"

"Newspapers! What on earth would we want them for? If we should need them at any time there are thousands of old ones piled up. But what is in them, anyway; only things that *happen*, wars and accidents and work and death. When these went newspapers went too. Listen," continued the Man in Asbestos, "you seem to have been something of a social reformer, and yet you don't understand the new life at all. You don't understand how completely all our burdens have disappeared. Look at it this way. How used your people to spend all the early part of their lives?"

"Why," I said, "our first fifteen years or so were spent in getting education."

"Exactly," he answered; "now notice how we improved on all that. Education in our day is done by surgery. Strange that in your time nobody realized that education was simply a surgical operation. You hadn't the sense to see that what you really did was to slowly remodel, curve and convolute the inside of the brain by a long and painful mental operation. Everything learned was reproduced in a physical difference to the brain. You knew that, but you didn't see the full consequences. Then came the invention of surgical education—the simple system of opening the side of the skull and engrafting into it a piece of prepared brain. At first, of course, they had to use, I suppose, the brains of dead people, and that was ghastly"—here the Man in Asbestos shuddered like a leaf—"but very soon they found how to make moulds that did just as well. After that it was a mere nothing; an operation of a few minutes would suffice to let in poetry or foreign languages or history or anything else that one cared to have. Here, for instance," he added, pushing back the hair at the side of his head and showing a scar beneath it, "is the mark where I had my spherical trigonometry let in. That was, I admit, rather painful, but other things, such as English poetry or history, can be inserted absolutely with the least suffering. When I think of your painful, barbarous methods of education through the ear, I shudder at it. Oddly enough, we have found lately that for a great many things there is no need to use the head. We lodge them—things like philosophy and metaphysics, and so on—in what used to be the digestive apparatus. They fill it admirably."

He paused a moment. Then went on:

"Well, then, to continue, what used to occupy your time and effort after your education?"

"Why," I said, "one had, of course, to work, and then, to tell the truth, a great part of one's time and feeling was devoted toward the other sex, towards falling in love and finding some woman to share one's life."

"Ah," said the Man in Asbestos, with real interest. "I've heard about your arrangements with the women, but never quite understood them. Tell me; you say you selected some woman?"

"Yes."

"And she became what you called your wife?"

"Yes, of course."

"And you worked for her?" asked the Man in Asbestos in astonishment.

"Yes."

"And she did not work?"

"No," I answered, "of course not."

"And half of what you had was hers?"

"Yes."

"And she had the right to live in your house and use your things?"

"Of course," I answered.

"How dreadful!" said the Man in Asbestos. "I hadn't realized the horrors of your age till now."

He sat shivering slightly, with the same timid look in his face as before.

Then it suddenly struck me that of the figures on the street, all had looked alike.

"Tell me," I said, "are there no women now? Are they gone too?"

"Oh, no," answered the Man in Asbestos, "they're here just the same. Some of those are women. Only, you see, everything has been changed now. It all came as part of their great revolt, their desire to be like the men. Had that begun in your time?"

"Only a little," I answered; "they were beginning to ask for votes and equality."

"That's it," said my acquaintance, "I couldn't think of the word. Your women, I believe, were something awful, were they not? Covered with feathers and skins and dazzling colours made of dead things all over them? And they laughed, did they not, and had foolish teeth, and at any moment they could inveigle you into one of those contracts! Ugh!"

He shuddered.

"Asbestos," I said (I knew no other name to call him), as I turned on him in wrath, "Asbestos, do you think that those jelly-bag Equalities out on the street there, with their ash-barrel suits, can be compared for one moment with our unredeemed, unreformed, heaven-created, hobble-skirted women of the twentieth century?"

Then, suddenly, another thought flashed into my mind—

"The children," I said," where are the children? Are there any?"

"Children," he said, "no! I have never heard of there being any such things for at least a century. Horrible little hobgoblins they must have been! Great big faces, and cried constantly! And *grew*, did they not? Like funguses! I believe they were longer each year than they had been the last, and——"

I rose.

"Asbestos!" I said, "this, then, is your coming Civilization, your millennium. This dull, dead thing, with the work and the burden gone out of life, and with them all the joy and the sweetness of it. For the struggle—mere stagnation, and in place of danger and death, the dull monotony of security and the horror of an unending decay! Give me back," I cried, and I flung wide my arms to the dull air, "the old life of danger and stress, with its hard toil and its bitter chances, and its heartbreaks. I see its value! I know its worth! Give me no rest," I cried aloud——

"Yes, but give a rest to the rest of the corridor!" cried an angered voice that broke in upon my exultation.

Suddenly my sleep had gone.

I was back again in the room of my hotel, with the hum of the wicked, busy old world all about me, and loud in my ears the voice of the indignant man across the corridor.

"Quit your blatting, you infernal blather-skite," he was calling. "Come down to earth."

I came.

A CATALOGUE OF SELECTED DOVER BOOKS
IN ALL FIELDS OF INTEREST

A CATALOGUE OF SELECTED DOVER BOOKS
IN ALL FIELDS OF INTEREST

AMERICA'S OLD MASTERS, James T. Flexner. Four men emerged unexpectedly from provincial 18th century America to leadership in European art: Benjamin West, J. S. Copley, C. R. Peale, Gilbert Stuart. Brilliant coverage of lives and contributions. Revised, 1967 edition. 69 plates. 365pp. of text.
21806-6 Paperbound $3.00

FIRST FLOWERS OF OUR WILDERNESS: AMERICAN PAINTING, THE COLONIAL PERIOD, James T. Flexner. Painters, and regional painting traditions from earliest Colonial times up to the emergence of Copley, West and Peale Sr., Foster, Gustavus Hesselius, Feke, John Smibert and many anonymous painters in the primitive manner. Engaging presentation, with 162 illustrations. xxii + 368pp.
22180-6 Paperbound $3.50

THE LIGHT OF DISTANT SKIES: AMERICAN PAINTING, 1760-1835, James T. Flexner. The great generation of early American painters goes to Europe to learn and to teach: West, Copley, Gilbert Stuart and others. Allston, Trumbull, Morse; also contemporary American painters—primitives, derivatives, academics—who remained in America. 102 illustrations. xiii + 306pp.
22179-2 Paperbound $3.00

A HISTORY OF THE RISE AND PROGRESS OF THE ARTS OF DESIGN IN THE UNITED STATES, William Dunlap. Much the richest mine of information on early American painters, sculptors, architects, engravers, miniaturists, etc. The only source of information for scores of artists, the major primary source for many others. Unabridged reprint of rare original 1834 edition, with new introduction by James T. Flexner, and 394 new illustrations. Edited by Rita Weiss. 6⅝ x 9⅝.
21695-0, 21696-9, 21697-7 Three volumes, Paperbound $13.50

EPOCHS OF CHINESE AND JAPANESE ART, Ernest F. Fenollosa. From primitive Chinese art to the 20th century, thorough history, explanation of every important art period and form, including Japanese woodcuts; main stress on China and Japan, but Tibet, Korea also included. Still unexcelled for its detailed, rich coverage of cultural background, aesthetic elements, diffusion studies, particularly of the historical period. 2nd, 1913 edition. 242 illustrations. lii + 439pp. of text.
20364-6, 20365-4 Two volumes, Paperbound $6.00

THE GENTLE ART OF MAKING ENEMIES, James A. M. Whistler. Greatest wit of his day deflates Oscar Wilde, Ruskin, Swinburne; strikes back at inane critics, exhibitions, art journalism; aesthetics of impressionist revolution in most striking form. Highly readable classic by great painter. Reproduction of edition designed by Whistler. Introduction by Alfred Werner. xxxvi + 334pp.
21875-9 Paperbound $2.50

ALPHABETS AND ORNAMENTS, Ernst Lehner. Well-known pictorial source for decorative alphabets, script examples, cartouches, frames, decorative title pages, calligraphic initials, borders, similar material. 14th to 19th century, mostly European. Useful in almost any graphic arts designing, varied styles. 750 illustrations. 256pp. 7 x 10.   21905-4 Paperbound $4.00

PAINTING: A CREATIVE APPROACH, Norman Colquhoun. For the beginner simple guide provides an instructive approach to painting: major stumbling blocks for beginner; overcoming them, technical points; paints and pigments; oil painting; watercolor and other media and color. New section on "plastic" paints. Glossary. Formerly *Paint Your Own Pictures*. 221pp.   22000-1 Paperbound $1.75

THE ENJOYMENT AND USE OF COLOR, Walter Sargent. Explanation of the relations between colors themselves and between colors in nature and art, including hundreds of little-known facts about color values, intensities, effects of high and low illumination, complementary colors. Many practical hints for painters, references to great masters. 7 color plates, 29 illustrations. x + 274pp.
                                                          20944-X Paperbound $2.50

THE NOTEBOOKS OF LEONARDO DA VINCI, compiled and edited by Jean Paul Richter. 1566 extracts from original manuscripts reveal the full range of Leonardo's versatile genius: all his writings on painting, sculpture, architecture, anatomy, astronomy, geography, topography, physiology, mining, music, etc., in both Italian and English, with 186 plates of manuscript pages and more than 500 additional drawings. Includes studies for the Last Supper, the lost Sforza monument, and other works. Total of xlvii + 866pp. 7⅞ x 10¾.
                                   22572-0, 22573-9 Two volumes, Paperbound $10.00

MONTGOMERY WARD CATALOGUE OF 1895. Tea gowns, yards of flannel and pillow-case lace, stereoscopes, books of gospel hymns, the New Improved Singer Sewing Machine, side saddles, milk skimmers, straight-edged razors, high-button shoes, spittoons, and on and on . . . listing some 25,000 items, practically all illustrated. Essential to the shoppers of the 1890's, it is our truest record of the spirit of the period. Unaltered reprint of Issue No. 57, Spring and Summer 1895. Introduction by Boris Emmet. Innumerable illustrations. xiii + 624pp. 8½ x 11⅝.
                                                          22377-9 Paperbound $6.95

THE CRYSTAL PALACE EXHIBITION ILLUSTRATED CATALOGUE (LONDON, 1851). One of the wonders of the modern world—the Crystal Palace Exhibition in which all the nations of the civilized world exhibited their achievements in the arts and sciences—presented in an equally important illustrated catalogue. More than 1700 items pictured with accompanying text—ceramics, textiles, cast-iron work, carpets, pianos, sleds, razors, wall-papers, billiard tables, beehives, silverware and hundreds of other artifacts—represent the focal point of Victorian culture in the Western World. Probably the largest collection of Victorian decorative art ever assembled— indispensable for antiquarians and designers. Unabridged republication of the Art-Journal Catalogue of the Great Exhibition of 1851, with all terminal essays. New introduction by John Gloag, F.S.A. xxxiv + 426pp. 9 x 12.
                                                          22503-8 Paperbound $4.50

AGAINST THE GRAIN (A REBOURS), Joris K. Huysmans. Filled with weird images, evidences of a bizarre imagination, exotic experiments with hallucinatory drugs, rich tastes and smells and the diversions of its sybarite hero Duc Jean des Esseintes, this classic novel pushed 19th-century literary decadence to its limits. Full un-abridged edition. Do not confuse this with abridged editions generally sold. Intro-duction by Havelock Ellis. xlix + 206pp. 22190-3 Paperbound $2.00

VARIORUM SHAKESPEARE: HAMLET. Edited by Horace H. Furness; a landmark of American scholarship. Exhaustive footnotes and appendices treat all doubtful words and phrases, as well as suggested critical emendations throughout the play's history. First volume contains editor's own text, collated with all Quartos and Folios. Second volume contains full first Quarto, translations of Shakespeare's sources (Belleforest, and Saxo Grammaticus), Der Bestrafte Brudermord, and many essays on critical and historical points of interest by major authorities of past and present. Includes details of staging and costuming over the years. By far the best edition available for serious students of Shakespeare. Total of xx + 905pp. 21004-9, 21005-7, 2 volumes, Paperbound $5.25

A LIFE OF WILLIAM SHAKESPEARE, Sir Sidney Lee. This is the standard life of Shakespeare, summarizing everything known about Shakespeare and his plays. Incredibly rich in material, broad in coverage, clear and judicious, it has served thousands as the best introduction to Shakespeare. 1931 edition. 9 plates. xxix + 792pp. (USO) 21967-4 Paperbound $3.75

MASTERS OF THE DRAMA, John Gassner. Most comprehensive history of the drama in print, covering every tradition from Greeks to modern Europe and America, including India, Far East, etc. Covers more than 800 dramatists, 2000 plays, with biographical material, plot summaries, theatre history, criticism, etc. "Best of its kind in English," *New Republic*. 77 illustrations. xxii + 890pp. 20100-7 Clothbound $7.50

THE EVOLUTION OF THE ENGLISH LANGUAGE, George McKnight. The growth of English, from the 14th century to the present. Unusual, non-technical account presents basic information in very interesting form: sound shifts, change in grammar and syntax, vocabulary growth, similar topics. Abundantly illustrated with quota-tions. Formerly *Modern English in the Making*. xii + 590pp. 21932-1 Paperbound $3.50

AN ETYMOLOGICAL DICTIONARY OF MODERN ENGLISH, Ernest Weekley. Fullest, richest work of its sort, by foremost British lexicographer. Detailed word histories, including many colloquial and archaic words; extensive quotations. Do not con-fuse this with the Concise Etymological Dictionary, which is much abridged. Total of xxvii + 830pp. 6½ x 9¼. 21873-2, 21874-0 Two volumes, Paperbound $5.50

FLATLAND: A ROMANCE OF MANY DIMENSIONS, E. A. Abbott. Classic of science-fiction explores ramifications of life in a two-dimensional world, and what happens when a three-dimensional being intrudes. Amusing reading, but also use-ful as introduction to thought about hyperspace. Introduction by Banesh Hoffmann. 16 illustrations. xx + 103pp. 20001-9 Paperbound $1.00

DESIGN BY ACCIDENT; A BOOK OF "ACCIDENTAL EFFECTS" FOR ARTISTS AND DESIGNERS, James F. O'Brien. Create your own unique, striking, imaginative effects by "controlled accident" interaction of materials: paints and lacquers, oil and water based paints, splatter, crackling materials, shatter, similar items. Everything you do will be different; first book on this limitless art, so useful to both fine artist and commercial artist. Full instructions. 192 plates showing "accidents," 8 in color. viii + 215pp. 8⅜ x 11¼. 21942-9 Paperbound $3.50

THE BOOK OF SIGNS, Rudolf Koch. Famed German type designer draws 493 beautiful symbols: religious, mystical, alchemical, imperial, property marks, ῑnes, etc. Remarkable fusion of traditional and modern. Good for suggestions of timelessness, smartness, modernity. Text. vi + 104pp. 6⅛ x 9¼. 20162-7 Paperbound $1.25

HISTORY OF INDIAN AND INDONESIAN ART, Ananda K. Coomaraswamy. An unabridged republication of one of the finest books by a great scholar in Eastern art. Rich in descriptive material, history, social backgrounds; Sunga reliefs, Rajput paintings, Gupta temples, Burmese frescoes, textiles, jewelry, sculpture, etc. 400 photos. viii + 423pp. 6⅜ x 9¾. 21436-2 Paperbound $3.50

PRIMITIVE ART, Franz Boas. America's foremost anthropologist surveys textiles, ceramics, woodcarving, basketry, metalwork, etc.; patterns, technology, creation of symbols, style origins. All areas of world, but very full on Northwest Coast Indians. More than 350 illustrations of baskets, boxes, totem poles, weapons, etc. 378 pp. 20025-6 Paperbound $2.50

THE GENTLEMAN AND CABINET MAKER'S DIRECTOR, Thomas Chippendale. Full reprint (third edition, 1762) of most influential furniture book of all time, by master cabinetmaker. 200 plates, illustrating chairs, sofas, mirrors, tables, cabinets, plus 24 photographs of surviving pieces. Biographical introduction by N. Bienenstock. vi + 249pp. 9⅞ x 12¾. 21601-2 Paperbound $3.50

AMERICAN ANTIQUE FURNITURE, Edgar G. Miller, Jr. The basic coverage of all American furniture before 1840. Individual chapters cover type of furniture—clocks, tables, sideboards, etc.—chronologically, with inexhaustible wealth of data. More than 2100 photographs, all identified, commented on. Essential to all early American collectors. Introduction by H. E. Keyes. vi + 1106pp. 7⅞ x 10¾. 21599-7, 21600-4 Two volumes, Paperbound $7.50

PENNSYLVANIA DUTCH AMERICAN FOLK ART, Henry J. Kauffman. 279 photos, 28 drawings of tulipware, Fraktur script, painted tinware, toys, flowered furniture, quilts, samplers, hex signs, house interiors, etc. Full descriptive text. Excellent for tourist, rewarding for designer, collector. Map. 146pp. 7⅞ x 10¾. 21205-X Paperbound $2.00

EARLY NEW ENGLAND GRAVESTONE RUBBINGS, Edmund V. Gillon, Jr. 43 photographs, 226 carefully reproduced rubbings show heavily symbolic, sometimes macabre early gravestones, up to early 19th century. Remarkable early American primitive art, occasionally strikingly beautiful; always powerful. Text. xxvi + 207pp. 8⅜ x 11¼. 21380-3 Paperbound $3.00

CATALOGUE OF DOVER BOOKS

EAST O' THE SUN AND WEST O' THE MOON, George W. Dasent. Considered the best of all translations of these Norwegian folk tales, this collection has been enjoyed by generations of children (and folklorists too). Includes True and Untrue, Why the Sea is Salt, East O' the Sun and West O' the Moon, Why the Bear is Stumpy-Tailed, Boots and the Troll, The Cock and the Hen, Rich Peter the Pedlar, and 52 more. The only edition with all 59 tales. 77 illustrations by Erik Werenskiold and Theodor Kittelsen. xv + 418pp. 22521-6 Paperbound $3.00

GOOPS AND HOW TO BE THEM, Gelett Burgess. Classic of tongue-in-cheek humor, masquerading as etiquette book. 87 verses, twice as many cartoons, show mischievous Goops as they demonstrate to children virtues of table manners, neatness, courtesy, etc. Favorite for generations. viii + 88pp. 6½ x 9¼.
22233-0 Paperbound $1.25

ALICE'S ADVENTURES UNDER GROUND, Lewis Carroll. The first version, quite different from the final Alice in Wonderland, printed out by Carroll himself with his own illustrations. Complete facsimile of the "million dollar" manuscript Carroll gave to Alice Liddell in 1864. Introduction by Martin Gardner. viii + 96pp. Title and dedication pages in color. 21482-6 Paperbound $1.00

THE BROWNIES, THEIR BOOK, Palmer Cox. Small as mice, cunning as foxes, exuberant and full of mischief, the Brownies go to the zoo, toy shop, seashore, circus, etc., in 24 verse adventures and 266 illustrations. Long a favorite, since their first appearance in St. Nicholas Magazine. xi + 144pp. 6⅝ x 9¼.
21265-3 Paperbound $1.50

SONGS OF CHILDHOOD, Walter De La Mare. Published (under the pseudonym Walter Ramal) when De La Mare was only 29, this charming collection has long been a favorite children's book. A facsimile of the first edition in paper, the 47 poems capture the simplicity of the nursery rhyme and the ballad, including such lyrics as I Met Eve, Tartary, The Silver Penny. vii + 106pp. 21972-0 Paperbound $1.25

THE COMPLETE NONSENSE OF EDWARD LEAR, Edward Lear. The finest 19th-century humorist-cartoonist in full: all nonsense limericks, zany alphabets, Owl and Pussycat, songs, nonsense botany, and more than 500 illustrations by Lear himself. Edited by Holbrook Jackson. xxix + 287pp. (USO) 20167-8 Paperbound $1.75

BILLY WHISKERS: THE AUTOBIOGRAPHY OF A GOAT, Frances Trego Montgomery. A favorite of children since the early 20th century, here are the escapades of that rambunctious, irresistible and mischievous goat—Billy Whiskers. Much in the spirit of Peck's Bad Boy, this is a book that children never tire of reading or hearing. All the original familiar illustrations by W. H. Fry are included: 6 color plates, 18 black and white drawings. 159pp. 22345-0 Paperbound $2.00

MOTHER GOOSE MELODIES. Faithful republication of the fabulously rare Munroe and Francis "copyright 1833" Boston edition—the most important Mother Goose collection, usually referred to as the "original." Familiar rhymes plus many rare ones, with wonderful old woodcut illustrations. Edited by E. F. Bleiler. 128pp. 4½ x 6⅜. 22577-1 Paperbound $1.25

"ESSENTIAL GRAMMAR" SERIES

All you really need to know about modern, colloquial grammar. Many educational shortcuts help you learn faster, understand better. Detailed cognate lists teach you to recognize similarities between English and foreign words and roots—make learning vocabulary easy and interesting. Excellent for independent study or as a supplement to record courses.

ESSENTIAL FRENCH GRAMMAR, Seymour Resnick. 2500-item cognate list. 159pp.
(EBE) 20419-7 Paperbound $1.25

ESSENTIAL GERMAN GRAMMAR, Guy Stern and Everett F. Bleiler. Unusual shortcuts on noun declension, word order, compound verbs. 124pp.
(EBE) 20422-7 Paperbound $1.25

ESSENTIAL ITALIAN GRAMMAR, Olga Ragusa. 111pp.
(EBE) 20779-X Paperbound $1.25

ESSENTIAL JAPANESE GRAMMAR, Everett F. Bleiler. In Romaji transcription; no characters needed. Japanese grammar is regular and simple. 156pp.
21027-8 Paperbound $1.25

ESSENTIAL PORTUGUESE GRAMMAR, Alexander da R. Prista. vi + 114pp.
21650-0 Paperbound $1.25

ESSENTIAL SPANISH GRAMMAR, Seymour Resnick. 2500 word cognate list. 115pp.
(EBE) 20780-3 Paperbound $1.25

ESSENTIAL ENGLISH GRAMMAR, Philip Gucker. Combines best features of modern, functional and traditional approaches. For refresher, class use, home study. x + 177pp.
21649-7 Paperbound $1.25

A PHRASE AND SENTENCE DICTIONARY OF SPOKEN SPANISH. Prepared for U. S. War Department by U. S. linguists. As above, unit is idiom, phrase or sentence rather than word. English-Spanish and Spanish-English sections contain modern equivalents of over 18,000 sentences. Introduction and appendix as above. iv + 513pp.
20495-2 Paperbound $2.00

A PHRASE AND SENTENCE DICTIONARY OF SPOKEN RUSSIAN. Dictionary prepared for U. S. War Department by U. S. linguists. Basic unit is not the word, but the idiom, phrase or sentence. English-Russian and Russian-English sections contain modern equivalents for over 30,000 phrases. Grammatical introduction covers phonetics, writing, syntax. Appendix of word lists for food, numbers, geographical names, etc. vi + 573 pp. 6⅛ x 9¼.
20496-0 Paperbound $3.00

CONVERSATIONAL CHINESE FOR BEGINNERS, Morris Swadesh. Phonetic system, beginner's course in Pai Hua Mandarin Chinese covering most important, most useful speech patterns. Emphasis on modern colloquial usage. Formerly *Chinese in Your Pocket.* xvi + 158pp.
21123-1 Paperbound $1.50

POEMS OF ANNE BRADSTREET, edited with an introduction by Robert Hutchinson. A new selection of poems by America's first poet and perhaps the first significant woman poet in the English language. 48 poems display her development in works of considerable variety—love poems, domestic poems, religious meditations, formal elegies, "quaternions," etc. Notes, bibliography. viii + 222pp.
22160-1 Paperbound $2.00

THREE GOTHIC NOVELS: THE CASTLE OF OTRANTO BY HORACE WALPOLE; VATHEK BY WILLIAM BECKFORD; THE VAMPYRE BY JOHN POLIDORI, WITH FRAGMENT OF A NOVEL BY LORD BYRON, edited by E. F. Bleiler. The first Gothic novel, by Walpole; the finest Oriental tale in English, by Beckford; powerful Romantic supernatural story in versions by Polidori and Byron. All extremely important in history of literature; all still exciting, packed with supernatural thrills, ghosts, haunted castles, magic, etc. xl + 291pp.
21232-7 Paperbound $2.00

THE BEST TALES OF HOFFMANN, E. T. A. Hoffmann. 10 of Hoffmann's most important stories, in modern re-editings of standard translations: Nutcracker and the King of Mice, Signor Formica, Automata, The Sandman, Rath Krespel, The Golden Flowerpot, Master Martin the Cooper, The Mines of Falun, The King's Betrothed, A New Year's Eve Adventure. 7 illustrations by Hoffmann. Edited by E. F. Bleiler. xxxix + 419pp.
21793-0 Paperbound $2.50

GHOST AND HORROR STORIES OF AMBROSE BIERCE, Ambrose Bierce. 23 strikingly modern stories of the horrors latent in the human mind: The Eyes of the Panther, The Damned Thing, An Occurrence at Owl Creek Bridge, An Inhabitant of Carcosa, etc., plus the dream-essay, Visions of the Night. Edited by E. F. Bleiler. xxii + 199pp.
20767-6 Paperbound $1.50

BEST GHOST STORIES OF J. S. LEFANU, J. Sheridan LeFanu. Finest stories by Victorian master often considered greatest supernatural writer of all. Carmilla, Green Tea, The Haunted Baronet, The Familiar, and 12 others. Most never before available in the U. S. A. Edited by E. F. Bleiler. 8 illustrations from Victorian publications. xvii + 467pp.
20415-4 Paperbound $2.50

THE TIME STREAM, THE GREATEST ADVENTURE, AND THE PURPLE SAPPHIRE—THREE SCIENCE FICTION NOVELS, John Taine (Eric Temple Bell). Great American mathematician was also foremost science fiction novelist of the 1920's. *The Time Stream*, one of all-time classics, uses concepts of circular time; *The Greatest Adventure*, incredibly ancient biological experiments from Antarctica threaten to escape; The *Purple Sapphire*, superscience, lost races in Central Tibet, survivors of the Great Race. 4 illustrations by Frank R. Paul. v + 532pp.
21180-0 Paperbound $3.00

SEVEN SCIENCE FICTION NOVELS, H. G. Wells. The standard collection of the great novels. Complete, unabridged. *First Men in the Moon, Island of Dr. Moreau, War of the Worlds, Food of the Gods, Invisible Man, Time Machine, In the Days of the Comet.* Not only science fiction fans, but every educated person owes it to himself to read these novels. 1015pp.
20264-X Clothbound $5.00

TWO LITTLE SAVAGES; BEING THE ADVENTURES OF TWO BOYS WHO LIVED AS INDIANS AND WHAT THEY LEARNED, Ernest Thompson Seton. Great classic of nature and boyhood provides a vast range of woodlore in most palatable form, a genuinely entertaining story. Two farm boys build a teepee in woods and live in it for a month, working out Indian solutions to living problems, star lore, birds and animals, plants, etc. 293 illustrations. vii + 286pp.

20985-7 Paperbound $1.95

PETER PIPER'S PRACTICAL PRINCIPLES OF PLAIN & PERFECT PRONUNCIATION. Alliterative jingles and tongue-twisters of surprising charm, that made their first appearance in America about 1830. Republished in full with the spirited woodcut illustrations from this earliest American edition. 32pp. 4½ x 6⅜.

22560-7 Paperbound $1.00

SCIENCE EXPERIMENTS AND AMUSEMENTS FOR CHILDREN, Charles Vivian. 73 easy experiments, requiring only materials found at home or easily available, such as candles, coins, steel wool, etc.; illustrate basic phenomena like vacuum, simple chemical reaction, etc. All safe. Modern, well-planned. Formerly *Science Games for Children*. 102 photos, numerous drawings. 96pp. 6⅛ x 9¼.

21856-2 Paperbound $1.25

AN INTRODUCTION TO CHESS MOVES AND TACTICS SIMPLY EXPLAINED, Leonard Barden. Informal intermediate introduction, quite strong in explaining reasons for moves. Covers basic material, tactics, important openings, traps, positional play in middle game, end game. Attempts to isolate patterns and recurrent configurations. Formerly *Chess*. 58 figures. 102pp. (USO) 21210-6 Paperbound $1.25

LASKER'S MANUAL OF CHESS, Dr. Emanuel Lasker. Lasker was not only one of the five great World Champions, he was also one of the ablest expositors, theorists, and analysts. In many ways, his Manual, permeated with his philosophy of battle, filled with keen insights, is one of the greatest works ever written on chess. Filled with analyzed games by the great players. A single-volume library that will profit almost any chess player, beginner or master. 308 diagrams. xli x 349pp.

20640-8 Paperbound $2.50

THE MASTER BOOK OF MATHEMATICAL RECREATIONS, Fred Schuh. In opinion of many the finest work ever prepared on mathematical puzzles, stunts, recreations; exhaustively thorough explanations of mathematics involved, analysis of effects, citation of puzzles and games. Mathematics involved is elementary. Translated by F. Göbel. 194 figures. xxiv + 430pp. 22134-2 Paperbound $3.00

MATHEMATICS, MAGIC AND MYSTERY, Martin Gardner. Puzzle editor for Scientific American explains mathematics behind various mystifying tricks: card tricks, stage "mind reading," coin and match tricks, counting out games, geometric dissections, etc. Probability sets, theory of numbers clearly explained. Also provides more than 400 tricks, guaranteed to work, that you can do. 135 illustrations. xii + 176pp.

20338-2 Paperbound $1.50

THE RED FAIRY BOOK, Andrew Lang. Lang's color fairy books have long been children's favorites. This volume includes Rapunzel, Jack and the Bean-stalk and 35 other stories, familiar and unfamiliar. 4 plates, 93 illustrations x + 367pp.
21673-X Paperbound $1.95

THE BLUE FAIRY BOOK, Andrew Lang. Lang's tales come from all countries and all times. Here are 37 tales from Grimm, the Arabian Nights, Greek Mythology, and other fascinating sources. 8 plates, 130 illustrations. xi + 390pp.
21437-0 Paperbound $1.95

HOUSEHOLD STORIES BY THE BROTHERS GRIMM. Classic English-language edition of the well-known tales — Rumpelstiltskin, Snow White, Hansel and Gretel, The Twelve Brothers, Faithful John, Rapunzel, Tom Thumb (52 stories in all). Translated into simple, straightforward English by Lucy Crane. Ornamented with headpieces, vignettes, elaborate decorative initials and a dozen full-page illustrations by Walter Crane. x + 269pp.
21080-4 Paperbound $1.75

THE MERRY ADVENTURES OF ROBIN HOOD, Howard Pyle. The finest modern versions of the traditional ballads and tales about the great English outlaw. Howard Pyle's complete prose version, with every word, every illustration of the first edition. Do not confuse this facsimile of the original (1883) with modern editions that change text or illustrations. 23 plates plus many page decorations. xxii + 296pp.
22043-5 Paperbound $2.00

THE STORY OF KING ARTHUR AND HIS KNIGHTS, Howard Pyle. The finest children's version of the life of King Arthur; brilliantly retold by Pyle, with 48 of his most imaginative illustrations. xviii + 313pp. 6⅛ x 9¼.
21445-1 Paperbound $2.00

THE WONDERFUL WIZARD OF OZ, L. Frank Baum. America's finest children's book in facsimile of first edition with all Denslow illustrations in full color. The edition a child should have. Introduction by Martin Gardner. 23 color plates, scores of drawings. iv + 267pp. 20691-2 Paperbound $1.95

THE MARVELOUS LAND OF OZ, L. Frank Baum. The second Oz book, every bit as imaginative as the Wizard. The hero is a boy named Tip, but the Scarecrow and the Tin Woodman are back, as is the Oz magic. 16 color plates, 120 drawings by John R. Neill. 287pp. 20692-0 Paperbound $1.75

THE MAGICAL MONARCH OF MO, L. Frank Baum. Remarkable adventures in a land even stranger than Oz. The best of Baum's books not in the Oz series. 15 color plates and dozens of drawings by Frank Verbeck. xviii + 237pp.
21892-9 Paperbound $2.00

THE BAD CHILD'S BOOK OF BEASTS, MORE BEASTS FOR WORSE CHILDREN, A MORAL ALPHABET, Hilaire Belloc. Three complete humor classics in one volume. Be kind to the frog, and do not call him names . . . and 28 other whimsical animals. Familiar favorites and some not so well known. Illustrated by Basil Blackwell. 156pp. (USO) 20749-8 Paperbound $1.25

MATHEMATICAL PUZZLES FOR BEGINNERS AND ENTHUSIASTS, Geoffrey Mott-Smith. 189 puzzles from easy to difficult—involving arithmetic, logic, algebra, properties of digits, probability, etc.—for enjoyment and mental stimulus. Explanation of mathematical principles behind the puzzles. 135 illustrations. viii + 248pp.
20198-8 Paperbound $1.25

PAPER FOLDING FOR BEGINNERS, William D. Murray and Francis J. Rigney. Easiest book on the market, clearest instructions on making interesting, beautiful origami. Sail boats, cups, roosters, frogs that move legs, bonbon boxes, standing birds, etc. 40 projects; more than 275 diagrams and photographs. 94pp.
20713-7 Paperbound $1.00

TRICKS AND GAMES ON THE POOL TABLE, Fred Herrmann. 79 tricks and games— some solitaires, some for two or more players, some competitive games—to entertain you between formal games. Mystifying shots and throws, unusual caroms, tricks involving such props as cork, coins, a hat, etc. Formerly *Fun on the Pool Table.* 77 figures. 95pp.
21814-7 Paperbound $1.00

HAND SHADOWS TO BE THROWN UPON THE WALL: A SERIES OF NOVEL AND AMUSING FIGURES FORMED BY THE HAND, Henry Bursill. Delightful picturebook from great-grandfather's day shows how to make 18 different hand shadows: a bird that flies, duck that quacks, dog that wags his tail, camel, goose, deer, boy, turtle, etc. Only book of its sort. vi + 33pp. 6½ x 9¼.
21779-5 Paperbound $1.00

WHITTLING AND WOODCARVING, E. J. Tangerman. 18th printing of best book on market. "If you can cut a potato you can carve" toys and puzzles, chains, chessmen, caricatures, masks, frames, woodcut blocks, surface patterns, much more. Information on tools, woods, techniques. Also goes into serious wood sculpture from Middle Ages to present, East and West. 464 photos, figures. x + 293pp.
20965-2 Paperbound $2.00

HISTORY OF PHILOSOPHY, Julián Marías. Possibly the clearest, most easily followed, best planned, most useful one-volume history of philosophy on the market; neither skimpy nor overfull. Full details on system of every major philosopher and dozens of less important thinkers from pre-Socratics up to Existentialism and later. Strong on many European figures usually omitted. Has gone through dozens of editions in Europe. 1966 edition, translated by Stanley Appelbaum and Clarence Strowbridge. xviii + 505pp.
21739-6 Paperbound $3.00

YOGA: A SCIENTIFIC EVALUATION, Kovoor T. Behanan. Scientific but non-technical study of physiological results of yoga exercises; done under auspices of Yale U. Relations to Indian thought, to psychoanalysis, etc. 16 photos. xxiii + 270pp.
20505-3 Paperbound $2.50

Prices subject to change without notice.
Available at your book dealer or write for free catalogue to Dept. GI, Dover Publications, Inc., 180 Varick St., N. Y., N. Y. 10014. Dover publishes more than 150 books each year on science, elementary and advanced mathematics, biology, music, art, literary history, social sciences and other areas.